Essentials
for Biblical
Preaching

DATE DUE

Essentials for Biblical Preaching

An Introduction to Basic Sermon Preparation

Al Fasol

BAKER BOOK HOUSE
Grand Rapids, Michigan 49516

To
Beverly,
Robert,
Vivian,
and
Malinda

whose love provides inspiration

Contents

Preface

Becoming an effective preacher is an intense challenge. Consider, for example, that a best-selling author is expected by publishers and readership to turn out one quality volume every three to five years. But a preacher (who usually prepares and delivers two sermons a week forty to fifty times per annum) speaks the equivalent of several medium-sized volumes every year. And preachers are expected to be creative and fresh on each of those Sundays!

A truly biblical sermon nourishes the growth of faith in the hearts of its hearers as applied in the power of the Holy Spirit, for ". . . faith cometh by hearing, and hearing by the word of God" (Rom. 10:17, KJV). It is the special privilege of a preacher to be instrumental in nurturing this growth in faith. However, just as Moses hesitated at the burning bush and Martin Luther trembled at the altar, every preacher knows something of the awesome responsibility inherent in God's call to be his spokesman. Yet the one truly called as an ambassador of the Lord also knows the inexpressible joy that arises from delivering the message, proclaiming the revelation, and heralding the Good News of the gospel.

Good volumes on preaching abound. *This* volume was planned as a primer to introduce the beginning preacher, whether professional or lay, to basic instruction in biblical preaching. Unlike more comprehensive books and volumes that treat a specific type of preaching in detail, this work seeks to enable the reader to face with confidence some of the basic challenges of sermon preparation.

This book was written primarily for preachers. The lessons taught in the book, however, are readily applicable to Bible study group teachers, Sunday church teachers, for preparing devotional talks, or for any form of communication which seeks to instruct or inspire someone to either become a Christian or to grow as a Christian.

One of the aims of this book is to lead preachers to base their sermons on a biblical text and not to use the text only as a springboard to launch into diatribes of personal opinion without authentic exposition of divine revelation.

Essentials for Biblical Preaching takes the novitiate pulpiteer step by step through an understanding of the spiritual attitude and mental processes of the person who preaches, to a grasp of the basic proclamation task, and finally into mastery of sermon-preparation specifics.

Unless otherwise noted, Scripture references are from the New International Version.

I am indebted to students from my classes throughout over fifteen years of teaching introductory preaching courses for insights I have gained while preparing them to respond in full measure to their calling. I also owe much to faculty colleagues and outstanding preachers whose needs and skills raised probing questions—the answers to which I now crystallize herein. Some have contributed directly, others have graciously reviewed and evaluated these materials. Nancy Owen and Barbara Walker labored long and hard at the technical tasks of manuscript preparation.

I thank all my "helpers." But primarily I thank God for giving me the exciting opportunity of proclaiming his Word. Into that very challenging and most satisfying of worlds I now invite you also to enter.

I take responsibility for the contents of this book, including any errors that might be mine. My prayer is that through these pages you may overhear the call of God to preach his truth as you discover with me how basic understandings and practical skills can be mastered for this highest of vocations.

Grasping the Fundamentals 1

Biblical Roots

There is no doubt that preaching is a biblically mandated activity. The biblical roots of preaching date back first to Hebrew prophecy and then to the Christian commission to spread the gospel. Early Hebrew prophecy as a specific calling dates back to the time of Moses although God's spokesmen certainly appeared before then. The divine office of the prophet is defined for us in Deuteronomy 18:14–22 (especially v. 18):

> The nations you will dispossess listen to those who practice sorcery or divination. But as for you, the LORD your God has not permitted you to do so. The LORD your God will raise up for you a prophet like me from among your own brothers. You must listen to him. For this is what you asked of the LORD your God at Horeb on the day of the assembly when you said, "Let us not hear the voice of the LORD our God nor see this great fire anymore, or we will die." The LORD said to me: "What they say is good. *I will raise up for them a prophet like you from among their brothers; I will put my words in his mouth, and he will tell them everything I command him.* If anyone does not listen to my words that the prophet speaks in my name, I myself will call him to account. But a prophet who presumes to speak in my name anything I have not commanded him to

say, or a prophet who speaks in the name of other gods, must
be put to death." You may say to yourselves, "How can we know
when a message has not been spoken by the LORD?" If what a
prophet proclaims in the name of the LORD does not take place
or come true, that is a message the LORD has not spoken. That
prophet has spoken presumptuously. Do not be afraid of him.

The "prophet" or preacher is one whom the Lord "will raise
up," or call. A divinely authorized prophet compels a hearing:
"You must listen to him," because, "I [the Lord] will put my
words in his mouth. . . ." There is no need to wonder how the
Lord really feels about preaching, for he has said, "If anyone
does not listen to my words that the prophet speaks in my
name, I myself will call him to account." Preaching—and listening to preaching—has always been an awesome responsibility and will continue to be.

A few homileticians cite Nehemiah 8:8 as the inaugural of
preaching as we understand it today: "They [the appointed
ones] read from the book of the law of God making it clear
and giving the meaning so that the people could understand
what was being read." This passage describes what we do as
preachers; that is, we announce a text, give its meaning and
bring about understanding and application to contemporary
life of the text. Evidently a form of this worship practice continued to the time of Jesus, when it was customary in the
synagogue for one or more men to read a passage of Scripture
and comment on it. Jesus himself exercised this privilege (cf.
Luke 4:16–21).

In the New Testament, several different words are employed
in reference to preaching. The most frequently used is *keryssein,* which means "to proclaim" but is usually translated
"to preach." *Keryssein* could also be translated "to herald," a
rare term these days, but it may be a more accurate rendering
since it denotes that the "herald" ("preacher") has a message
that was sent or authorized by another.

Another New Testament word for preaching is *euangeli-
zesthai,* which means "to bring good tidings or good news."

This was the word used, for instance, by the angel in Luke 2:10 ". . . 'Do not be afraid. I bring you good news of great joy, that will be for all people.' " Other words referring to preaching include: *didaskein* (to teach divine truths), *dialegesthai* (to dialogue or discourse with another person with a view to persuasion), *parabalein* (to admonish with a view to moving another person to your point of view), and *lalein* (to talk or to discourse).

"Preaching" in the New Testament therefore covers a wide variety of activities, including proclamation before an assembly of people and public discourse just short of a debate. Such a discourse could seek to answer questions or respond to comments, as Paul did on Mars Hill (Acts 17:16–33) or in Ephesus (Acts 19). Or preaching could occur in private conversations ("witnessing"), which might occur spontaneously during the daily events of life or within the context of a specific visitation plan.

Definitions

The variety of biblical words for "preaching" and the differing situations in which this activity arose hardly allow for a concise definition of the term. This, however, has not hindered many from offering definitions, especially within the last hundred years. For one of the briefest definitions of preaching we can thank the famed Episcopalian preacher Phillips Brooks. While lecturing on preaching at Yale Divinity School in 1877, Brooks said, "Preaching is the communication of truth by man to men. It has in it two essential elements, truth and personality. Neither of those can it spare and still be preaching."[1] Brooks's ten-word description seems irreducible. Any good definition of preaching cannot exclude "truth" (the Bible) communicated by a "personality" (the preacher) to other "personalities" (the congregation, for example).

These definitions encompass the varied activities in the Bible referred to as preaching. Brooks's basic definition could also refer to teaching a Sunday school lesson, to sharing a personal Christian testimony, or to witnessing through conversing with another person (cf. Acts 8:26–38). Preaching is a multifaceted activity that is difficult to define except in broad terms. For our purposes, we will specify that *preaching is orally communicating truth as found in the Bible in a way that applies God's Word to life today.* The purpose or goal of preaching is to elicit a positive response to the biblical message.

Historical Backgrounds

Christian preaching has a fascinating history that has generally been divided into eight distinct eras.

1. *The Patristic Era* (70–430). This period is usually subdivided into 70–300 and 300–430. In addition, E. C. Dargan has categorized the preaching of this era into three classes: the Apostolic Fathers, the Apologists, and the Theologians.[2]

The time between A.D. 70 and A.D. 300 required major adjustments for Christians. Persecution of Christians steadily intensified, Jerusalem was destroyed, the Roman Empire continued its expansion and the apostolic period came to a close. All this profoundly affected preaching. After the first apostles died, their disciples became the primary preachers. Some were known as Apostolic Fathers, including Ignatius, Polycarp, and Clement of Rome. Other preaching notables, the Apologists, included Justin Martyr and Tertullian. Toward the end of the second century the Theologians—Origen, Clement of Alexandria, Irenaeus, and Hippolytus—were hailed as powerful preachers.

The later years (300–430) yielded magnificent preaching. Christianity now had the sanction of the state. Renowned preachers of this period were Basil, Gregory of Nyssa, Gregory of Nazianzen, Ambrose, Hilary, Augustine, and perhaps the greatest of this era, Chrysostom.

The prevailing sermon form of the Patristic Era was the homily, or running commentary on Scripture (often imprecisely referred to today as expository preaching). Most sermons were informal, personal, simple and direct.[3]

2. *The Dark Ages* (430–1095). Preaching suffered enormously during this arid period in Christian history. The pathos of these bleak times is aptly described in *Steps to the Sermon:*

> Preachers were corrupt; the liturgy strangled the power of the pulpit; the sacerdotal spirit grew until the preacher became the priest. Doctrinal controversies became common in the face of mounting corruption of doctrine. From without, hordes of barbarians came storming into the Christian world. Fanaticism and superstition abounded; the worship of angels, saints, relics, and Mary replaced the worship of Christ. Preachers were ignorant and drunk on perverted allegory.[4]

Despite the spiritual illness of the Dark Ages, five names stand out like beacons. Bede, Patrick, Gall, Boniface, and Eligius preached as effectively as was possible during this sad millennium in western church history.

3. *The Scholastic Era* (1095–1361). A spiritual renewal within Christendom began with a healthy sense of mysticism and a fresh desire for scholasticism. These trends resulted partly from the Crusades, which brought the Western World in touch with the advanced culture of the Middle East and the Orient. Although the Crusades were an unhappy chapter in church history, multitudes joined the religious warfare in response to the power of certain speechmakers. Peter the Hermit and Theodore the Penniless aroused thousands to march on the Holy Land. This eloquence was noticed by such saintly men as Francis of Assisi and Dominic, who established preaching orders to take on missionary endeavors. Interest in preaching revived accordingly.

4. *The Reformation Era* (1361–1572). (The pre-Reformation age is designated as 1361–1517, and the Reformation Age as 1517–1572.) After Francis and Dominic died, preaching declined once more. As in the Dark Ages, only a few voices

stood out. Men like John Wycliffe, John Huss, and Savonarola were forerunners of the Protestant Reformation.

The Reformation brought a significant revival of preaching. The use of the Bible became especially prominent in the preaching of Luther, Calvin, Zwingli, and Knox. As the pulpit regained a central place in worship, the Bible became the sole authority for preaching. Brown, Clinard, and Northcutt summarized this trend:

> . . . the leaders (of the Reformation) made preaching of the Word central in their task. After a thousand years of being relegated to a secondary role behind the Mass, preaching emerged as the most effective method for proclaiming God's good news. . . . The pulpit was central; the sermon was in the language of the people; and the Bible was the supreme authority for the spoken messages. The reformers recognized, practiced, and taught that preaching was the primary function of a minister of the Lord Jesus Christ.[5]

5. *The Post-Reformation Era* (1572–1700). These years comprise the classic era of preaching in both France and England. In France, King Louis XIV especially enjoyed listening to preachers. The Edict of Nantes in 1598 provided religious toleration of French Calvinists—the Huguenots—and encouraged the development of such gifted men as Bossuet, Bourdaloue, Fenelon, and Massillon.

In England, the Authorized Version of the Bible (King James Version, 1611) stirred interest in God's Word as well as in preaching. Richard Baxter, John Bunyan, John Donne, and Jeremy Taylor were the especially notable preachers. Sermons of this era were pleasingly balanced with biblical exposition, doctrine, and application to life.

6. *The Great Awakening* (1700–1800). The great evangelical revivals of the eighteenth century were led primarily by Jonathan Edwards, Theodore Frelinghuysen, Gilbert Tennent, George Whitefield, and John and Charles Wesley. The sermon structure of this period was informal and exhortative.

7. *The Era of Progress* (1800–1900). In general, this era was marked by advances in democratic forms of government, a new appreciation for science, the development of industry, the growth and termination of slavery in the Western World, the advancement in missionary endeavors, and increased church organization.

Several great churchmen represent the nineteenth century, which—like the first and fourth—was a showcase of excellence and power in Christian preaching. Prominent names of this period include: Charles H. Spurgeon, F. W. Robertson, Joseph Parker, Alexander MacLaren, John A. Broadus, Phillips Brooks, Henry Ward Beecher, T. DeWitt Talmadge, Dwight L. Moody, Charles G. Finney, and Horace Bushnell. Their preaching was characterized by vividness, sensory appeal, intensity, and logic.

8. *The Modern Era* (since 1900). Twentieth-century preaching has been profoundly influenced by Walter Rauschenbusch, Karl Barth, and Billy Graham, though only a later generation will be able to look back and assess this period of church history. Early findings indicate rapid and sometimes sensational church growth, increasing use of the electronic media for preaching, and growing ministerial attention to secondary spiritual concerns, such as pastoral counseling and charismatic expressions in worship. No doubt, some great preaching prevails today and these notable exceptions will be adequately recognized in the future.

Continuity

Amply documented is the importance of preaching in the Old Testament, in the New Testament, and in the rest of human history. Despite individual shortcomings, preaching persists as an integral part of Christian worship. Preaching has been both eulogized and derided on many occasions, but it has always survived its critics.

The art of preaching prevails in spite of human frailties.

For every preacher who commanded unusual eloquence, a thousand others lacked it. For every Chrysostom, Fenelon, John Jasper, and Billy Graham there are thousands of less gifted but nonetheless dedicated preachers of the Word of God. Many preachers with only moderate skills have been loved and appreciated by those to whom they minister in word and act. Preaching, fortunately, has never had to rely solely on the oratory skills of the practitioner for its success or its survival.

Preaching has persistently survived its charlatans, who have ranged from the sons of Sceva (Acts 19:15) to contemporary cult leaders. There is no human way to measure the damage that deceivers have caused by casting suspicions on all preachers. Despite these tricksters, however, there are millions of witnesses to the veracity of preaching when delivered by a faithful minister of the Word.

Preaching has endured envy and strife since the first century. As Paul testified,

> "It is true that some preach Christ out of envy and rivalry, but others out of good will. . . . The former preach Christ out of selfish ambition, not sincerely. . . . But what does it matter? The important thing is that. . . . whether from false motives or true, Christ is preached. And because of this I rejoice . . ." (Phil. 1:15, 17–18).

Today there is no lack of mixed motives behind the proclamation of the Good News. Pretense, jealousy, strife, contention, and insincerity overlay good will and sincerity—but preaching still survives.

"Preaching" (as defined earlier in this chapter) prevails in spite of those who would re-create its delivery techniques. Almost every generation has had at least one progenitor of a "new way" to preach. Some have suggested that preaching be done in a dialogue. Others force preaching into either the mold of a Madison Avenue commercial, the style of psychological counseling, or the format of an entertainment program. Preaching nonetheless survives attempts to re-create it through a radically new look.

Clyde Fant has aptly concluded:

> No part of the worship service has been so generously and ecumenically roasted as preaching, but likewise no aspect of its worship has been so generally . . . practical . . . . Preaching . . . has a double stubbornness: it is stubbornly the same, and it is stubbornly there."[6]

Basic Premises

At least two presuppositions are basic to authentic preaching:

1. *The Bible is authoritative for preaching.* The Bible must be accepted as the Word of God—the "word" to which Paul referred Timothy when he wrote, "Preach the Word . . ." (2 Tim. 4:2).

Although the literary devices, chronology, and historicity of the Bible have been discussed and debated among Christians (especially since the Reformation), for the majority of believers there is no question as to the Scriptures' "divine inspiration." Most "official" church confessions since the Reformation include a clear statement on the inspiration of Scripture, and many include the Bible in the first article of the confession. For example, the Second Hebretic confession of 1566 opens with these words: "We believe and confess the Canonical Scriptures of the holy prophets and apostles of both Testaments to be the true Word of God. . . . The Second London (Baptist) Confession of 1677 began with this assertion about the Bible: "The Holy Scripture is the only sufficient, certain, and infallible rule of all saving Knowledge, Faith, and Obedience. . . ."

Questions regarding the extent and the form of inspiration are still debated. John Newport and William Cannon summarized the debate in a 1974 publication:

> Some groups state that the Bible is infallible in all matters. Others say it is infallible only for faith and practice. Some argue that the Bible teaches a clear doctrine of verbal inspiration.

Others affirm that a less dogmatic and more inductive approach to inspiration should be followed. In recent years a very controversial approach to the Bible has been the "Neo-Orthodox" view. Karl Barth and Emil Brunner, as well as other of its exponents, reacted against traditional orthodoxy. The orthodox view maintained that revelation was given as verbally inspired and communicated doctrine to the minds of the writers of the Bible. This the Neo-Orthodox rejected. For them, revelation is primarily an event—not a doctrine, nor a book. For the Neo-Orthodox, the Bible is a record of revelation, not the revelation itself.[7]

2. *Biblical truth should be proclaimed by a spiritually prepared person.* Since Christian preaching is based on the biblical text, a primary requisite for the preacher is a thorough knowledge and ongoing study of the Bible. The best way to grow in scriptural knowledge is by reading the Bible, of course. But it might amaze us to know how many preachers have never read the Bible from Genesis through Revelation. They may have read various books about the Bible and studied certain books of the Bible in their entirety, but never read the whole Bible. Reading the Bible through provides basic insights that no preacher should be without. Cover-to-cover reading gives one a feel for how the various books of the Bible are arranged, both topically as well as chronologically; how individual books relate to each other; and, very significantly, how the New Testament applies the Old Testament to teaching situations of the Christian era.

The preacher trained in Hebrew and Greek should read the Bible in its original languages. There are nuances in every language that are not (or cannot be) conveyed in a translation. Reading in the original languages helps the reader think as the original writers thought, and this is invaluable for a richer understanding of the Bible.

Obviously, not every preacher can read the Bible in its original languages. Many effective preachers have never been trained to read a Hebrew Old Testament or a Greek New Testament. For such preachers, numerous translating aids are available. Start with a Bible that is a "translation" rather than a mere "paraphrase." The New American Standard Bible is especially helpful in that regard because it provides marginal notes indicating either literal or other possible translations of a word or phrase. "Study editions" of other translations, such as the New International Version, also provide help with vocabulary interpretation. In addition, hundreds of Bible study aids—ranging from basic book-by-book summaries to finely detailed commentaries—include English translations of Hebrew and Greek words.

Another primary area of spiritual preparation is prayer. Since it is the Word of God being delivered and interpreted, a preacher obviously needs to be in communication with the Author. In sermon preparation, you should pray about your interpretation of the biblical text, about the people with whom you will share the Word of God, and for yourself as a preacher of that truth. As Spurgeon so appropriately put it: "The best and holiest men have made prayer the most important part of pulpit preparation."[8]

How much should you pray? Perhaps no one can set guidelines for this highly personal aspect of spiritual living. Paul testified that he prayed without ceasing. Some ministers of the Word have emphasized that we can never pray "too much." For many preachers, prayer is offered before, during, and after sermon preparation until the preacher feels, "I have reached the end of myself. I have neither the time nor the know-how for further preparation. I now turn this sermon over to God, praying that he who made the universe out of nothing can now empower and bless this sermon." Such a prayer usually brings a feeling of peace and release.

Prayer times should include periods of quiet meditation. Prayer does not have to be a constant verbalizing to God, either mentally, audibly, or in writing. Silence allows God to speak to us. Silence allows our minds time to grasp a new insight that God wants to insert into the mainstream of our thoughts.

A third area of spiritual preparation involves Christian fellowship, which occurs, of course, wherever Christians are gathered. This can be enjoyed at worship, at social events, in recreational activities, in ministerial meetings, in denominational conferences. The community of believers shares testimonies, points of view, questions, burdens, and victories. Fellowship may occasionally help to clarify opposing points of view. One man was heard to remark to another at a church dinner, "I understand and appreciate you now that we have our feet under the same table." Fellowship helps Christians experience a shared unity of purpose and a sense of spiritual uplifting that is rarely experienced in other gatherings and totally lacking in, for instance, the contemporary cocktail party.

A final aspect of spiritual preparation that is vital but often overlooked by preachers is physical fitness. An obese preacher, for example, needlessly experiences several unnecessary physical ailments that interfere with spiritual preparation. The very acts of breathing or of kneeling are compounded by being overweight. Among all the professions, that of the minister ranks among the highest in heart disease. The stereotype of a jolly, fat preacher may be pleasant and comforting, but any physician could tell you that rotund joviality is too often a terminal "disease." A group of children once dubbed all preachers "giant, walking marshmallows—they are very big, very soft, and very sugary." Physically fit persons may not be more spiritually healthy than anyone else, but they do have a greater capacity to enjoy their spiritual condition.

Ministerial Context

Preaching, although of primary importance, is but one of many roles that every so-called preacher must fulfill. The pastor/preacher, student/preacher, evangelist/preacher, counselor/preacher, denominational worker/preacher, lay preacher, and teacher/preacher all lead complex lives. Although preaching overlaps, complements, reciprocates, and enhances these multiple roles, most preachers consider communicating the

Word of God as their most important responsibility. On the other hand, most preachers are constantly pressured into spending less and less time in sermon preparation. How does a preacher juggle a multitude of responsibilities and still find time for adequate sermon preparation? Fortunately, a preacher can relate his or her various other responsibilities, in varying degrees, to preaching. Sermon insights can come in counseling sessions, visitations, administrating, and teaching, as well as in the office or study. Reciprocally, insights gained in sermon preparation may be used in counseling, visitation, administrative work, and teaching assignments. Everything the preacher does, no matter what the function may be, can fuel the preacher's mind for sermon preparation. Even in leisurely recreation or vacation periods the preacher's subconscious is at work. The only time wasted by a preacher is time spent in indolence.

Each preacher should develop a personalized daily and weekly schedule. One preacher works on sermons from 7:00 A.M. till 10:00 A.M. daily and spends the rest of the day in visitation, counseling, and administrative responsibilities. Another preacher finds it more productive to work on sermon preparation from 4:00 P.M. to 7:00 P.M. daily and handle other responsibilities earlier in the day. Study and sermon-preparation time require some shielding from phone calls and unscheduled visitors. Except for emergencies, no interruptions should be allowed during the time set aside for sermon preparation.

Is there a specific formula as to how much time should be spent in preparing each sermon? No! Whoever specified "one hour of sermon preparation for every minute of preaching" was at best idealistic. The preacher, however, should reserve enough time in a daily schedule of administrative duties, counseling, and pastoring to prepare for preaching. Each preacher needs to determine how much time he or she needs for "adequate" preparation.

The suggestions for sermon preparation submitted in this book may be very time-consuming at first, but after "walking through" the suggested disciplines, sermon preparation will constantly become easier and more expeditious. These suggestions can in no way teach anyone how to preach. The purpose is to expose and interpret the tools of effective preaching and then to rely on the preacher to refine them and develop his or her own craftsmanship and individual style in the preparation and delivery of biblical sermons.

Developing Relevant Themes 2

Where do preachers find ideas for their sermons? Traditionally, sermon ideas have been found in the Bible, in the needs of people, in personal experiences, in flashes of inspiration, in reading both secular and theological literature, in everyday life, and in planned programs of preaching. Ideas for sermons, therefore, are found almost anywhere. The two most prolific sources for sermon ideas, though, are the Bible and the needs of people.

Sources for Sermon Ideas

Bible-Based Sources

The Bible is the record of God's revelation of himself to humanity. This divine revelation provides a wonderfully varied library of historical record and narrative, drama, poetry, proverbs, correspondence, and apocalyptic literature. Much of the Scriptures tell the story of God as he meets people in the actual experiences of life. God has made himself known to people in their crises and triumphs, in their disappointments and aspirations. Since these stories were based in fact, the Bible has a message for life today. "The Bible as the message of life experiences with God is eternally contemporary. Its stories and its messages are always relevant."[1] The Bible is God's unique and full revelation to humanity today, just as it has been for centuries.

The Bible can serve as a source for sermon ideas in several ways, the most common of which is to let the biblical text directly suggest an idea. For instance, if the text deals with the Lordship of Christ, a sermon on Christ as Lord would be appropriate. If the text deals with loving one's neighbor, a sermon on applying this love in daily life would be appropriate. There are numerous biblical passages that almost instantly suggest an idea for a sermon. This would include such familiar passages as John 3:7; John 3:16; Romans 1:16; Romans 8:28; 1 Corinthians 13; Matthew 5:1–12; Matthew 5:13–16; Micah 6:6–8; John 14:1–6.

The biblical text also includes a wide variety of doctrines that can be developed into sermons. In a sense, the entire Bible is a set of doctrinal revelations. Some doctrines, however, may be more relevant to a contemporary congregation than others. Many pertinent sermons could be built on those portions of biblical text dealing with the sovereignty of God, the meaning and purpose of the Christian life, the second coming of Christ, and God's redeeming grace. Such preaching will challenge a congregation spiritually and intellectually.

Also, the Bible is full of stories about people—their struggles and their relationships to God and one another. Where there are people and their stories, there is a treasury of sermon ideas.

Finally, many preachers marvel that as they read the Bible devotionally and prayerfully—or just for the joy of reading it—sermon ideas occur to them constantly and spontaneously. As one preacher put it, "It is like a dream fishing trip—they are popping all around me and I hardly know where to cast next."

Discovering sermon ideas from the Bible is most likely to occur if the preacher balances devotional time with time spent in ministry to people. Finding sermonic direction from Scripture is less likely to occur if the Bible is simply "used" only as a source of texts to preach on—especially if this search is remote from daily life.

Sources Centering on Needs

For a preacher, therefore, awareness of the needs of people is almost as important as knowing the Bible. Samuel Shoemaker wrote, "Concrete human problems, and the Gospel answer, is the best starting place for sermons."[2] Following Brooks's statement about preaching ("truth communicated by man to men"), people are the "men" part of that definition. Concrete human problems and needs are discerned by contact with people in general, as well as by contact with members of the specific congregation for whom a sermon will be prepared.

Human contact comes from daily routines lived outside the study. Contact may be as formal and direct as organized visitation, which seeks to reach people who are not part of church life. Unchurched people often ask the kind of probing questions about life that can send a preacher back to his or her study to find answers. Although unchurched people usually hold fallacies about Christianity that need to be corrected, their insights are worth hearing. Such direct contact with other people often turns up some community or individual needs that should be addressed through preaching and pastoral care.

Members of a particular congregation express their concerns to preachers in a multitude of situations: in conversations in counseling sessions, and in church-related meetings. The sensitive preacher detects deep questions, such as: "What is the meaning of life?" Or "What is the meaning of evil and suffering?" Other concerns are more immediate: "How can I get along with my spouse?" Or "How can I relate better to my children?" Many persons are highly concerned about world hunger and other social issues. Others worry about the impact of cults or question the influence of what has become known as televangelism. Whenever feasible, the effective preacher addresses these concerns in a sermon.

Contact with people may also be on an indirect basis. One perceptive layman, Homer Buerlein, wrote:

> It's disappointing to see great events of national and inter-national importance go unnoticed from the pulpit because they don't conform to the lectionary. Although they may not be appropriate as the complete sermon topic, such monumental events as man walking on the moon, the release of hostages from Iran or Lebanon, the election of a new President of the United States, and Voyager II making its headlong flight into the regions of Jupiter and Saturn are worth mention. It takes only slight flexibility and creativity to incorporate happenings such as these in a sermon. *After all, they are important to listeners, and to include them indicates that the preacher shares their lives and interests* [italics mine].[3]

As Buerlein correctly asserts, citing recent worldwide, national, or local events adds credibility to preaching. The news media often reveal human needs that should be addressed from the pulpit in a spirit of Christian fellowship.

Sources Drawing on Personal Experience

Contact with people, obviously, generates many personal observations and experiences from which sermon ideas may emerge. Appropriate sermon ideas are usually the byproduct of pastoral care and love. Topics for sermons often come from personal spiritual victories that other people can share—an answered prayer, a surge of spiritual growth, or the joy of helping someone in his or her spiritual pilgrimage. Such experiences can reveal new insights into living as a Christian. These ideas could translate into major sermon themes—for example, on determining the will of God or on the value of patience in the Christian life.

Spiritual crises can also yield sermon ideas. For many spiritual giants, it was a crisis that eventually played a part in their becoming the faithful believers they were and are. Response to a handicap or to a wayward adolescent, a tragic accident, or a personal victory over temptation is part of the spiritual fabric of many outstanding Christians. A preacher's own soul is reflective of the needs of humanity in general. The more sensitivity preachers develop as they face their own spiritual victories and crises, the more sensitive they will become to the human needs that should be addressed in their sermons.

Preachers should guard against projecting themselves as spiritual super-humans who are untouched by the frailties and hurts and the joys and pleasures experienced by their congregations. The preacher is as human as any other person and must therefore lean on God in the struggles of life. Congregations are encouraged in knowing that their preachers personally share many of the same kind of problems that burden them. A message about God's love and guidance means much more to a congregation when preached by one who has experienced these blessings.

Spiritual insight can also occur unexpectedly in the little routines of daily life. Helmut Thielicke used such an experience as a brilliant introduction to a sermon based on a parable in Luke 15:11–24:

> Several years ago I once set my little son down in front of a large mirror. At first he did not recognize himself because he was still too young. He quite obviously enjoyed seeing the small image that smiled at him from this glass wall. But all of a sudden the expression on his little face changed as he began to recognize the similarity of the motions and he seemed to be saying, "That's me!"
>
> The same thing may happen to us when we hear this story. We listen to it at first as if it were an interesting tale with which we ourselves have nothing to do. A rather odd but fascinating fellow, this prodigal son. Undoubtedly true to life, undoubtedly a definite type of person whom we have all met at some time or other. And certainly we are all objective enough to feel a bit of sympathy with him.
>
> Until suddenly *our* face may change too, and we are compelled to say, "There I am, actually. This is I." All of a sudden we have identified the hero of this tale and now we can read

the whole story in the first person. Truly this is no small thrill. This is the way we must move back and forth until we have identified ourselves with the many people who surrounded Jesus. For as long as we fail to recognize *ourselves* in these people we fail to recognize the *Lord*.[4]

Inspirational Input

Flashes of inspiration catch you off guard, but you should be delighted they happen! Give these unannounced treasures special attention. When a flash of inspiration brightens your mind and heart, write it down immediately. Don't lose it by complacently thinking, "This is such a special moment that I will never forget it." Recording your flashes of inspiration makes them a part of you and opens your consciousness to other illuminations. If a sudden inspirational moment is unrecorded, it will usually leave as quickly as it came, likely never to return.

Flashes of inspiration will more likely occur to preachers who enjoy a variety of spiritually oriented activities: Bible study, contact with people, and personal meditation. The more enthusiastically a preacher participates in the various forms of ministry, the more frequently will inspiring input occur. These sudden insights are a lot like the kind of "good luck" that comes most often to those who are well prepared. Just like unexpected but welcome guests, the best flashes of inspiration visit the most receptive neighborhoods, and the best neighborhoods for inspiration are the minds of those already active in service to the Lord.

Reading Input

Reading in the theological disciplines is acutely important in developing an effective biblical sermon. All of the theological disciplines—biblical studies, archaeology, church history, philosophy, theology, ethics, missions, evangelism, counseling, and homiletics—are important resources for sermon preparation.

Other helpful subjects for the preacher's reading are: secular history (to be aware of the trends of human thought); biographies and autobiographies (to better understand human behavior); great literature (to benefit from the perceptive insights and the keen observations of gifted authors); and newspapers and news magazines (to keep on top of current events). These are only basic suggestions and can be expanded according to personal interests.

Input from Everyday Life

Effective preachers should also follow the example of Jesus by being involved in the everyday affairs of life. Jesus was trained as a carpenter. He was found frequently in marketplaces, sea shores, agricultural fields, on mountains, in synagogues, as well as at the temple. When Jesus spoke, he often made references to everyday items, such as a sower going out to sow, a man who lost a sheep, a woman who lost a coin, a rebellious son, the influence of leaven in bread, etc. In this way Jesus was constantly sensitive to ways to relate eternal truths to everyday life.

Ideas for sermons may be found almost anywhere, but the preacher must be sensitive to them. The process of discovering an idea for a sermon is greatly enhanced if the preacher is growing intellectually and emotionally. This growth will occur if the preacher is a constant student of all of the theological disciplines and an active participant in the everyday affairs of life.

Programmed Planning

A planned program of preaching is another valuable device for discovering sermon ideas. A survey of the church and/or secular calendar will alert you to special days. New Year's Day, Easter, Pentecost, Independence Day, Labor Day, Thanksgiving, and Christmas—each suggests its own theme. Christian Home Week, World Day of Prayer, and other designated times for church observances point to important emphases on the home, Christian missions, or national concerns. Awareness of dates, seasons, and the current needs of people can help in the planning of a special sermon or series of sermons.

Preaching Program (June–July)

June A.M. Services *Christ and Man*

June 3: "Christ and Searching Man" (Matt. 4:18–22)

June 10: "Christ and the Friendless Man" (Ps. 142:4)

June 17: (Father's Day) "Christ and the Family Man" (Mark 5:22–43)

June 24: "Christ and the Fragmented Man" (Mark 5:1–20)

June P.M. Services *Psalms*

June 3: Psalm 23—"God in Three Dimensions"

June 10: Psalm 73—"Our Footing and Our Faith"

June 17: Psalm 55—"Life: A Load or a Lift"

June 24: Psalm 103—"Lest We Forget"

July A.M. Services

July 1: (Independence Day) "Freedom Is Not Free" (John 8:11–36)

July 8: "Jesus at the First" (John 1:1–14)

July 15: "Jesus' First Sermon" (Mark 1:14–15)

July 22: "Jesus' First Miracle" (John 2:1–11)

July 29: "Jesus' First Disciples" (Mark 1:16–20)

July P.M. Services

July 1: Psalm 1—"Freedom's Tree" (Independence Day)

July 8: Psalm 46—"Our Only Line of Defense"

July 15: Psalm 121—"The Divine Bodyguard"

July 22: Psalm 139—"Living Exposed Lives"

July 29: Psalm 10—"The Sounds of Silence"

This preacher also annually reviewed his preaching emphases:

Areas of Sermonic Emphasis for the Year

The Bible—1

Development of the Christian Life—4

Doctrines (e.g. God, Christ, Holy Spirit—23)

Evangelism—10

Christian Home Life—5

Christian Morality—2

Christian Citizenship—2

The Church—2

Stewardship—4

Personal Faith—8

Textually Defining Sermon Topics

We have seen that there is a rich variety of sources for sermon ideas. However, finding a sermon idea is only the beginning. The next step is to relate the sermon idea to one or more specific biblical texts.

The word *text* (from the Latin word *textus*) implies "a web," since the verb root that most applies to this study is *texere*, meaning "to weave." The basic idea behind a biblical "text" is that it is a portion of Scripture that provides the basic threads from which the sermon is built, or woven.

Unfortunately, biblical texts are used (or rather abused) in many ways. Some preachers regard a biblical text simply as a peg from which various ideas are suspended like a string of paper clips. Other preachers painstakingly look for wording in a biblical text that either relates to or just seems to relate to a sermon idea they had in mind. Still others simply read a text, then abandon its content almost completely. They promote a philosophy of preaching that says, "Do not let the Bible interfere with your sermon." Obviously, a biblical text should never be disregarded or even adjusted to fit a predetermined sermon idea. Instead, the sermon idea should be adapted (or sacrificed, if necessary) to the parameters of the biblical text.

What is the proper length of a biblical text used as a basis for a sermon? This is not always easy to determine. Generally, the text should form a complete unit of thought in itself, usually, at least a paragraph or the main portion of a paragraph. Selected texts, however, might range in length from a single sentence (Matt. 5:3), to a chapter (a psalm), to several chapters (Job 12–14), to an entire book (Jonah, 3 John, or Jude). By aiming for a complete unit of thought in selecting a biblical text, the preacher greatly minimizes the possibility of misusing the Bible.

When the chosen text seems too long for development into just one sermon and/or for reading prior to the sermon, the preacher can exercise some options for reducing the length of the text to be applied to the sermon. The preacher could first orally summarize much of the textual material and then use a shorter portion of the Scripture as a focal passage. The key passage for Job 12–14, for example, could be 13:20–22. Another possibility is to read portions of the text as they are needed in various parts of the body of the sermon. For example, consider the division of 1 Kings 18–19 into these focal passages: 18:17–19; 20–24; 29; 38–39. These individual passages could be read aloud as the sermon progresses, while the rest of the text is orally summarized. Emphasizing certain passages can facilitate the development of a sermon and shorten the material selected for public reading.

The biblical text chosen as the basic fabric of the sermon need not be confined to just a single passage. The pertinent text may consist of one or more biblical passages related to a single topic or theme, although a single passage that forms a complete unit of thought is usually sufficient as the text for one sermon. In such cases another passage of Scripture should not be added. However, to make a general rule that no sermon should have more than one passage of Scripture as its text unnecessarily limits the ways a sermon can be developed and preached. Here is an example of how a multiple passage text might be used for a sermon:

Text: 1 John 3:8; John 19:28–30; 1 John 4:4

Title: "Why Jesus Came"

Outline

1. Jesus came to destroy sin (1 John 3:8).
2. Jesus came to offer Himself as an atonement (John 19:28–30).
3. Jesus came to empower us for victory against evil (1 John 4:4).

Authentically Anchored Preaching

Why should a sermon have a biblical text as its starting point? The first reason is the most obvious. Since a preacher's aim is to communicate the Word of God, the simplest way to do that is to take a portion of that Word and build the sermon on and around that section. Since the text is the basic raw material of a sermon, how could preaching possibly take place without a biblical focus?

Second, a text prevents the sermon from becoming merely

an editorial, or personal comment. Editorializing belongs only on the opinion page of a newspaper or magazine. Personal comment, which reflects no more than the preacher's own conclusions, must be labeled accordingly. Such conclusions *could* be biblical, but the authority of Scripture is no longer obvious. A sermon should seldom reflect anything but the thoughts and conclusions of the underlying text and its Author.

Third, using a text gives the sermon a point of reference: a direction or objective. Whichever term is applicable, the text charts a course for the sermon to follow. Texts are an inexhaustible source of sermon ideas. Any one text may have a specific, central idea that needs to be preached, but at the same time most texts have a number of secondary ideas that may be brought out in that sermon or may be a viable subject for a later one. As Lenski observed:

> Most texts can be preached on repeatedly with great profit. They are so full of life and power that one effort always leaves a great abundance of material for future use. This is due to the fact that the Scriptures are divine. No human book is like them. The last commentaries have not yet been written on even the smaller books of the Bible.[5]

Obviously, the mere announcement of a text reference does not guarantee an effective biblical sermon. Only God knows how often a biblical text has been ignored or abused rather than appropriately employed in preaching. Subsequent chapters of this book will demonstrate how preachers can prepare sermons in ways that limit subjectivism and misuse of a biblical text.

On rare occasions a sermon will not have a particular biblical text. Although such a sermon should allude to biblical principles or even use specific verses for explanatory purposes, a biblical text *per se* is not an absolute requirement. For instance, one preacher found that his series of sermons on the Christian family was meeting special needs in the congregation. He decided to expand the series, and one added sermon was to deal with modern dating and courtship. Of course he could find no passage of Scripture that related specifically to contemporary practices in these areas. Rather than choose a text that had a remote or vague connection to the subject, he began by saying, "Although I believe that most sermons should be based on a biblical text, I found none for the sermon I am about to preach." Then he explained why. Although the preacher did rely on biblical principles for this sermon, he did not misuse the Bible by forcing a biblical text onto his message. He not only preached a sermon every young person needs to hear but demonstrated how a good Bible-based sermon could be preached without using a specific textual focus.

Although sermon ideas can be obtained in various ways and from many different sources, finding just the right idea for a specific sermon—perhaps an everyday situation—can be a problem. Once an idea is crystallized, however, the topic must be related at least indirectly to a biblical text of one or more passages. At that point, the text dictates the development of the sermon and not the other way around. The ultimate truth of God's Word demands that a text be used for proper purposes, one of which is to underlay and support the sermon built on its elements.

Interpreting the Text

3

Making an accurate interpretation of the biblical text is as vital as anything else the preacher does in preparing a sermon. John A. Broadus wrote: "To interpret and apply his text in accordance with its real meaning is one of the preacher's most sacred duties."[1] Interpretation of Scripture is the cornerstone not only of the entire sermon preparation process, but also of the preacher's life. A faithful student of Scripture will seek to be as certain as possible that the interpretation is biblically accurate.

It is important for us to acknowledge that the task of interpreting Scripture (technically known as hermeneutics) is inevitably colored by our presuppositions, opinions, culturally conditioned preferences and prejudices, unique experiences, and individual gifts and talents. These subjective factors begin literally at birth and influence our actions, thinking, and emotions to varying degrees thereafter. It is important, therefore, for us to acknowledge these early impressions developed through family life, Christian role models, and various life experiences, since they can either help or hinder our interpretation of Scripture. For some of us, this individual conditioning has produced rigid dogmatism, while others of us approach the interpretation of Scripture with flexibility and open-mindedness. All of us must sift through our subjectivity as much as we can and allow the Bible to speak rather than imposing our own views on the text. To accomplish this we will attempt, later in this chapter, to devise a method of interpretation that minimizes our subjectivity.

Biblical interpretation is also largely influenced by our view of the nature of Scripture. This author's faith presupposition is that even though the available biblical manuscripts are not the originals and do include textual variations, and even though God chose to use human instruments to write the biblical books, these manuscripts are nonetheless totally reliable and authoritative for our faith and practice (2 Tim. 3:16). This whole issue of the nature of the Bible is so important that we are compelled to give it a cursory study.

Critical Studies of the Bible

Studies of the extant manuscripts of the Bible have taken four general directions: textual criticism, source criticism, form criticism, and redaction criticism. Whether or not a preacher is interested in using the evidence of these studies, he or she should be aware of them. The positive use of the words *criticism* or *critical* is analogous to what we imply when we say, "He has a *critical decision* to make regarding his future." That is, this person has to make *extremely important evaluations* so that he can come to a correct decision. At their best, critical studies of the Bible seek not to diminish the Bible but to improve our understanding of it.

In *textual criticism,* scholars seek to determine the one authentic reading of a specific passage of Scripture from among the differing readings found in the various manuscripts. As a case in point, the *textus receptus,* from which the King James Version was translated, contains the Greek word *teleious* in 1 Corinthians 1:8 and is translated "blameless." In the same verse, another manuscript, P46, contains the word *teleous* which is rendered "mature" or "complete." Which manuscript is accurate?

Such answers, obviously, are of varying degrees of importance to a preacher. Some are crucial, some less significant. Thousands of manuscripts and manuscript fragments are now available, compounding the task of textual critics. For some passages, the majority of manuscripts may have the same textual reading, and a decision about the rendering can thus be made with some confidence. However, if a minority reading has a textual variation that appears only in the *older* manuscripts, this lends the minority reading a strong measure of credibility. Textual-critical decisions cannot be made easily or lightly. A conscientious biblical preacher will welcome any insights that textual criticism may provide.

Source criticism relates in particular to the New Testament books of Matthew, Mark, and Luke, the so-called Synoptic Gospels. A source critic compares these three Gospel accounts as to similarities and differences in reporting the same incident. Matthew 5, for example, refers to a sermon on the *mount;* Luke 6 refers to probably the same sermon as occurring on the *plain.* The source critic seeks the original source of information from which these accounts came.

Harold Freeman notes the value of source criticism for the preacher:

> If approached properly, the use of a harmony of the gospels can be productive for preaching. The harmony should be used, not with the view to resolving the differences, but with a view to discovering them and discerning them as significant components of a larger work with an overarching theme. The harmony should not be an effort to synchronize chronology but to recognize the distinctive theology of the Gospels. When we recognize the Evangelist's intent, constituent parts of the book come into sharper focus. For example, it may be of more than passing interest that the parable of the Good Samaritan in Luke 10 is preceded by the account in Luke 9 of Jesus' rebuke of James and John for their anger at the inhospitable Samaritan village. It is perhaps significant that both of these accounts with a "Samaritan" focus occur only in the gospel of Luke. This is even more interesting in the light of the gentile Luke's purpose to show Jesus as a universal Savior, in contrast

to Matthew's purpose to show him as the Messiah. How many sermons have been preached on the parable of the Good Samaritan! How few sermons have been preached on the incident about the Samaritan village? Could it be that the point of the Good Samaritan parable is more profound than a general moralism defining a neighbor as anyone in need? Could the overarching concept be that God is the God of all? Then, perhaps, the record of the incident at the Samaritan village also has more than passing interest as a mere incident in the life of Jesus.[2]

Another type of critical study is *form criticism* which probes the oral traditions assumed to have preceded the written documents. Form critics hold the view that certain accounts first appeared orally, then were written, and finally these materials were utilized by the biblical writers. One of the basic premises of the form critic is that the literary form in the Bible—be it parable, narrative, or sermon—was shaped by the earlier form of the passage in question.

Why is this important from the standpoint of preaching? First, this knowledge leads us to a more accurate determination of what constitutes a text for a sermon, and prevents us from fragmenting or proof-texting a passage. Second, it is much easier to interpret a text properly if we understand its literary form.

A fourth category, *redaction criticism,* evaluates Scripture relative to why and how the biblical materials are arranged. The redaction critic presumes that the biblical author had a particular theology in mind as he selected the materials to be used. The redaction critic states, for example, that Matthew looked on Jesus as the promised Messiah and thus arranged his materials around that theme. On the other hand, Mark based his writings on a servant-Messiah theology and arranged his material accordingly. The redaction critic, then, studies the Bible with a view to determining how the theology of the author affected the arrangement and use of material.

Knowing the theology of an author or the purpose the writer

had in mind can often be of tremendous benefit to the biblical preacher in interpreting a text. Care should be taken, however, not to deviate too far from the text itself, especially if one is not an "expert" in redaction-critical methodology.

History of Biblical Interpretation

A brief look at the history of biblical interpretation will help us as we prepare our own hermeneutical approach.

The Apostolic Perspective

Christian interpretation of Scripture begins, obviously, with Jesus himself. Jesus often quoted directly from the Hebrew Bible and added an interpretation. For example, Jesus quoted Isaiah 29:13 to describe his adversaries: " 'Those people honor me with their lips, but their hearts are far from me. They worship me in vain; their teachings are but rules taught by men' " (Matt. 15:8–9; Mark 7:6–7). This is an interpretation of Scripture, since Jesus was applying a verse written centuries earlier to a particular situation in his own ministry.

Jesus also interpreted Scripture by elaboration. In one section of his Sermon on the Mount, Jesus began a series of antithetical statements by saying, "You have heard . . . but I tell you . . ." (Matt. 5:21–46). Jesus' interpretive emphases were on broad moral issues and personal relations rather than on blind obedience. This approach is illustrated in Jesus' interpretation of the Sabbath and ritual cleansing (Mark 7:1–23).

Jesus set forth important principles for us in his interpretation of Scripture. We, too, must be true to the spirit of the text being interpreted even as we make strong, relevant, and accurate applications to our own day. On the other hand, a thorough study of Jesus' methods also teaches us to be nei-

ther slavishly devoted to rigid roles of interpretation nor swayed
by current expository fads.

During the apostolic period, Jesus' interpretive methodology was reflected and expanded throughout the New Testament. A study of how Old Testament quotations were used in
the New helps us interpret Scripture today. In addition to recording verbatim quotes by Jesus, there were four ways in
which New Testament writers quoted the Old Testament:

1. *Quotes that are virtually verbatim.* Perhaps these were
quotes from memory and therefore not verbally precise; or
perhaps the New Testament writers were quoting from the
slightly different wording of the Greek translation of the Hebrew Bible, known as the Septuagint. As an example, note
that Romans 9:33 (cf. 10:11) quotes from Isaiah with a slight
variation from the Hebrew text. Isaiah 28:16 reads: "See, I lay
a stone in Zion, a tested stone, a precious cornerstone for a
sure foundation; the one who trusts will never be dismayed."
In Romans 9:33, Isaiah 26:18 is combined with Isaiah 8:14:
"See, I lay in Zion a stone that causes men to stumble and a
rock that makes them fall, and the one who trusts in him will
never be put to shame." The New Testament writer felt free to
interpret the original passage by personalizing the cornerstone (see also 1 Peter 2:6–8).

2. *Fragmentary quotations.* The New Testament writers
apparently believed that a fragment of a full quote was sufficient at times. (We need to remember, of course, that their
"manuscripts" did not have punctuation. Also, chapter-and-
verse divisions came centuries after the New Testament was
written.) For example, the author of Hebrews used fragmentary quotes in 1:5 (quoting Ps. 2:7), in 1:6 (quoting Deut.
32:43), in 2:12 (quoting Ps. 22:22), and in 2:13 (quoting Isa.
8:17–18).

Isaiah 8:17–18 reads:

> I will wait for the LORD, who is hiding his face from the house
> of Jacob. I will put my trust in him. Here am I, and the children

the LORD has given me. We are signs and symbols from Israel from the LORD Almighty, who dwells on Mount Zion.

Compare this with Hebrews 2:13:

And again, "I will put my trust in him." And again he says, "Here am I, and the children God has given me."

The author of Hebrews obviously felt free to select portions of the quotation from Isaiah to clarify to his readers Christ's humanity and dependency on God.

3. *Exegetical paraphrasing.* On several occasions a New Testament writer changed the wording of an Old Testament passage, apparently to underscore the meaning and intent of the Old Testament author. Thus, Stephen's quoting of Amos 5:25–27 (Acts 7:42–43) simply brings into perspective the real sense of the passage, which was the charge of idolatry. Similarly, Matthew (15:8–9) and Mark (7:6–7)—by paraphrasing—make a significant interpretation of Isaiah 29:13. This change brings out the prophet's thought more closely than a literal translation of the original Hebrew could. The Isaiah passage distinguished between a worship of God that was taught by men and the worship taught in God's Word. The New Testament writers revised the wording so as to make its meaning clearer in their day.

4. *Composite quotations.* In some instances the New Testament writers combined quotations from different sections of a book or even from several books. Matthew 21:13, Mark 11:17, and Luke 19:46 quote compositely from Isaiah 56:7 and Jeremiah 7:11. The theme of the prophets was the correct perception of the Temple and the composite quote blends perfectly to underscore this point without changing either passage.

Even though the New Testament writers were not always overly concerned with verbal precision, in no instance did they deliberately abuse, proof-text, distort, or mislead with their quotations of the Old Testament. They injected nothing really

new into their quotations, but instead took the spirit of the
Old Testament passage and gave it application suitable to their
readers. Modern preachers must be as conscientious as the
New Testament writers in their interpretation of Scripture.

The Allegorical Perspective

Allegory is a method of interpretation that gives a specific
word or phraseology a nonliteral meaning. The figurative (or
symbolic) meaning is determined by the interpreter. For example, Philo (a Jewish philosopher in the time of Jesus) used
allegory to reconcile the Hebrew Bible with Greek philosophy.
One way he accomplished this was by interpreting the four
rivers of the Garden of Eden as the classic virtues of prudence,
temperance, courage, and justice. Under what circumstances
would an interpreter use allegory? Biblical allegorists such as
Philo believe there is a deeper spiritual meaning hidden or at
least implied in a biblical passage which can be found only by
the use of allegory. In Christian circles, Clement (of Alexandria) and Origen were the first to popularize this method.
Clement taught that Scripture has three meanings: literal,
moral, and spiritual. The literal rendering was considered
mundane and elementary, whereas the spiritual sense con-
tained the deepest meaning.

There are disadvantages to allegorical interpretation. For
one, allegory can easily replace the intent of Scripture with
the subjective purposes of the interpreter. The four rivers of
Eden, for instance, could just as easily be called good deeds,
church attendance, loving attitudes, and warm fellowship. To
be used effectively, the allegorical approach must attempt to
communicate a message that is viable to its biblical text.

Creedal Perspective

The many conflicts about Scripture interpretation that arose
even in New Testament times made the idea of an authoritative creed appealing to believers. The radical simplicity of hav-
ing all questions of orthodoxy settled by a clear statement of

dogma still appeals to many Christians. The problems with creedal authority are obvious. First, a creed attempts to reduce the infinity of truth to possibly oversimplified formulas that our finite minds can handle. A creedal perspective also tends to make the creed as important as the Bible itself. Finally, a definitive statement of belief may stifle the pursuit of truth as the creed becomes too authoritative.

The value of a creed is that it gives us a common basis on which to discuss and pursue our insights into truth. When the creed is understood as a tool to increase our understanding of Scripture, it is valuable. When the creed is considered just as authoritative and binding as Scripture itself, it is an obstacle.

The Mystical Perspective

The mystical approach to biblical interpretation is similar to the use of allegory for exposition. Hugo (d. 1141) and Bernard of Clairvaux (d. 1153) are among the earliest commentators to use mysticism in interpreting Scripture, and their work revived allegorical thinking. Although, like the allegorists, Hugo and Bernard felt that the Scriptures had various depths of meaning, their mystical perspective was not as systematic as those who relied specifically on allegory. The mystics relied on what they called the "inner light" given by the Holy Spirit. This light supposedly revealed the true meaning of Scripture to the mystic. This approach, in varying ways and degrees, is still in use among interpreters today.

Whereas the strength of the mystical approach to Scripture lies in its reliance on the Holy Spirit, there is some danger in its frequently extreme subjectivity. It can become even more radical than allegory in bypassing the rules of grammar and natural word and usage in arriving at peculiar and superficial troubling interpretations.

The Rationalistic Perspective

Rationalistic interpretation generally asserts that the human mind is capable of determining the validity of anything purported to be "truth." There are several subdivisions in this school of interpretation when applied to the Bible: (1) myth-ism, which assumes that man created God through stories about Him; (2) naturalism, which rejects the supernatural "miracles" or divine intervention; and (3) moralism, which states that though the Bible is a good book for studying ethics, its theology is not important.

We can learn from rationalism to use our minds more fully. The chief problem with rationalism, however, is that it disa-vows the existence of God, rejects the supernatural acts of God, and discounts the authority of Scripture, while virtually deifying the human mind.

Contemporary Perspectives

The main divisions in the modern interpretive approach include neo-orthodoxy, demythologizing-existentialism, and the grammatical-historical-theological method.

1. *Neo-orthodoxy* generally accepts the Bible as authorita-tive, but not necessarily infallible. Neo-orthodoxy emphasizes the symbolic interpretation of Scripture, a focus that mini-mizes and at times even disregards the historical background of the Bible.

2. *Demythologizing-existentialism* seeks to understand Scripture only in its relevance to the life of the interpreter. "Myth" here means anything in Scripture that is incompatible with the modern scientific method and humanism.

3. *Grammatical-historical-theological methodology* seeks to interpret Scripture by using rules of grammar, historical information, and basic theological analysis. Careful gram-matical study helps the interpreter understand the meaning of the biblical text. Knowing the historical setting puts the Scripture in context. Basic theological analysis seeks to in-terpret Scripture by the rules of grammar against its historical background. This is the method we will seek to develop as our own hermeneutical approach.

Inductive Study

Our hermeneutical process is best begun by a repeated personal reading of the biblical text. (It is also important, especially on this first reading, to read the context of the text. The context includes the verses that come immediately before and after the text.) It is preferable that this reading begin with the original languages—primarily Hebrew in the Old Testament and Greek in the New. (More discussion of the value of reading a biblical text in its original language appears later in this chapter.) Whether or not such a reading is possible, the next step is to read the biblical text in a preferred and reliable version. The New American Standard Bible, the New International Version, the King James Version, and the Revised Standard Version are all considered commendable translations. Ideally, repeated readings from a favorite version should be interspersed with comparative readings from other translations. A "study edition" often features helpful explanatory material on difficult passages.

While translating and reading a biblical text, the preacher should make some observations and ask some questions. For example, in reading 1 Peter 1:3, the notations could be made as in Table 1.

These preliminary observations and questions are the first steps toward interpreting the text accurately. This process allows the interpreter to make personal observations before commentaries and study helps are consulted.

Deductive Study

The next step is to consult various interpretive works to arrive at the desired goal of the hermeneutical process: an *exegesis*. The root of this word means "to lead or guide out." An exegesis, as used here, is a detailed interpretation of an individual Bible passage. The general resources for an exegetical study include:

Critical commentaries (these deal with the structure and
nature of the language of the text)

Table 1

Text: 1 Peter 1:3 (NKJV)	Observations	Questions
Blessed be the God and Father of our Lord Jesus Christ,	Sounds like an emphatic statement. Perhaps an exclamation mark would be appropriate.	What does "blessed" mean in this context?
who according to His abundant mercy	"His" refers back specifically to "God and Father."	What does "according" mean?
has begotten us again	Note the reference to a second birth.	
to a living hope through the resurrection of Jesus Christ from the dead.	Our hope receives its life by means of Jesus' resurrection. Without the resurrection, there would be no hope.	"Hope" of what?

> *Devotional commentaries* (these focus on the introspective thoughts of the commentator)
>
> *Bible dictionaries*
>
> *Bible encyclopedias*
>
> *Bible handbooks*

These resources provide information that helps us to interpret a passage of Scripture. (A sample page of exegetical notes appears in Appendix A.) With these resources in hand, specific studies can be made in the following areas.

Literary Genre

The literary genre of a text tells us the literary form of the material to be interpreted. Different types of literature call for different interpretive approaches.

1. *Historical* books (e.g., Genesis, 2 Chronicles, Acts) are to be understood as mainly that—narratives of actual events. There are specialized books of history—the Prophets, the Gos-

pels, and the Epistles, some of which may be interpreted literally, at least in part. But a literal interpretation of even "historical" passages may sometimes be too simplistic an approach. Even if a passage is historical, it may also contain some figures of speech and poetic elements.

2. *Wisdom* literature is inspirational or instructive and may occur as poetry (Psalms), as maxims (Proverbs), or as a philosophical essay (Song of Songs, Ecclesiastes). The Book of Job utilizes prose, poetry, and essay styles. Wisdom books, which may contain generous symbolism, cannot be interpreted in the same way as historical narratives.

3. *Apocalyptic* literature—for example, Revelation—is extremely symbolic prophecy. The major challenge is to wade through the mystifying symbols to determine the message they are meant to convey. Not only must the interpreter discover the meaning of the symbols but must also decide whether any specific passages should be interpreted literally.

Historical Background

An understanding of the historical and cultural setting of a text is vital to understanding that text. History is such a broad subject that an interpreter usually needs to focus on specific aspects of the background material:

1. *Authorship.* A study of authorship is important in most textual analysis. Each biblical author wrote in the context of his personality, his environment, and his cultural conditioning. Matthew, for example, was a tax collector, a profession that most likely earned him the enmity of his countrymen. As a tax collector Matthew was accustomed to dealing with details. It is therefore not surprising that he would have kept detailed notes on the Sermon on the Mount, especially the Beatitudes, which emphasized comfort for those who were despised or rejected. Nor is it surprising that Matthew, a Jew, would seek to relate Old Testament prophecies to the coming of the Messiah.

2. *Dating.* The date a biblical book was written can also be

helpful in interpreting its contents since this information suggests its cultural context. This is often important for our understanding of a biblical text, especially when the specific teaching of a text is directed toward a pertinent cultural situation. For example, in 1 Corinthians 8, the problem of eating meat offered to idols had a definite cultural reference and Paul directed his remarks to that situation.

3. *Purpose.* A study of the purpose for writing can provide an important clue for interpreting a text. John is one of the few biblical writers who states his purpose: "But these are written that you may believe that Jesus is the Christ, the Son of God; and that by believing you may have life in his name" (John 20:31). The purpose of most other books of Scripture must be deduced. Once the purpose or occasion for writing the book is at least tentatively determined, the texts within that book can be more accurately interpreted. (A sample historical study appears in Appendix B.)

Lexical Information

Lexical, or vocabulary, resources yield a fascinating amount of information about a text. Since the meaning and usage of words are constantly changing, one of the challenges of the interpreter of Scripture is to find what a word meant at the particular time it was used. We should try to discover not only the word's denotative meaning (that is, how a dictionary defines the word), but also its connotation (that is, the impression, picture, feeling, or idea conveyed to people when they heard or read that word).

To better understand the lexical contribution to exegesis, we will first consider a few examples of the way the English language has changed and is still changing. In the years from 1675 to 1710, Christopher Wren, the noted English architect and engineer, was commissioned to build a cathedral. When the edifice was finally completed, Queen Anne gave it a thorough inspection. When she finished her tour of inspection, the queen announced, "I find this cathedral artificial, amusing, and awful!" Christopher Wren was delighted to hear this because in those days the word *artificial* meant full of art, the word *amusing* meant thought-provoking, and the word *awful* meant awe-inspiring. The same words used in description today would be considered insulting. This short tale points out why it is imperative that biblical interpretation takes into account the meaning of a word at the time it was used.

Next let us consider some biblical word studies. The Hebrew word *al-panaya* literally means "to my faces." *Al-panaya* is often translated "before," as in "You shall have no other gods before me" (Exod. 20:3). "To my faces" is a figure of speech implying that God can see everywhere, or God's face is everywhere. Therefore, we can understand this text to mean, "You shall have no other gods before [in front of] me, beside me, behind me, beneath me, or above me—there is no room *anywhere* in the universe for any other gods!" In this case, the lexical study of *al-panaya* increases the depth of our understanding of the verse.

The Greek word *opsonia* originally meant "cooked meat," which obviously does not offer an accurate rendering if so translated in Romans 6:23: "The cooked meat *[opsonia]* of sin is death. . . ." However, one first-century meaning of the word *opsonia* is "substitute pay." This makes much more sense: "The substitute pay of sin is death. . . ." Evidently, *opsonia* was "substitute pay" for money that had originally been promised. Again, thorough lexical study helps to provide an accurate interpretation of *opsonia* and enhances our understanding of the rest of the verse.

Grammatical Study

A study of the grammar of the original biblical languages is helpful for interpreting the text. As an example, consider John 19:30. "When he had received the drink, Jesus said, 'It is finished.' With that, he bowed his head and gave up his spirit." In the Greek, "It is finished" *(tetelestai)* is a verb in the perfect tense. The Greek perfect tense verb combines activity that is ongoing with activity that occurred at a given time. This means that we can interpret *tetelestai* to mean, "My mission is accomplished here on the cross and the results of this action will continue from now on." Knowing that *tetelestai* is a perfect tense verb adds to our understanding of what is meant by "It is finished."

Theological Resources

Theological insight is dependent on the study of context, and on the use of literary, historical, and lexical study aids. Here is where our research begins to bear fruit for preaching. There is no end to the variety and refinement of available theological devices for biblical interpretation, but—to narrow our scope of concern—we will consider here how to use a specific theological tool with reference to sermon preparation. The relationship between theology and preaching is like inhaling and exhaling—each one vital to the other. Theology provides a mass of information about our belief system. Preaching draws from this information and conveys it in a pertinent way to a contemporary congregation.

To relate a theological tool to sermon preparation, we will prepare the "Central Idea of the Text" (CIT), the "Major Objective of the Text" (MOT), the Thesis, and the Major Objective of the Sermon (MOS).

1. A CIT is a fifteen-to-eighteen-word (maximum) past-tense statement interpreting what the text meant then. To reemphasize, the CIT is an interpretive statement written in the past tense and specified as fifteen to eighteen words because that is a good length for a simple declarative sentence. It is stated in the past tense to force us as interpreters to involve ourselves in the setting in which the text was written. Biblical texts are too often interpreted as if the text had meaning *only* for the present time. The more we steep ourselves in the meaning (or meanings) of the text when it was written, the more intelligently we may deduce an eternal principle that also applies to today. The CIT is "interpretive" because a major func-

tion of preaching is to clarify a given text for a congregation. A simple restatement of the text is *not* a CIT.

2. The *Major Objective of the Text* (MOT) is a broad description of its primary purpose or intent. The MOT has two possible categories of concern: evangelistic and the Christian life.

3. The *Thesis* of a sermon is a fifteen-to-eighteen-word (maximum) present-tense application of the CIT. This is a critical step in interpretation. It is never enough just to know what the Bible meant *then;* we must always make application to *now.* Thus, the thesis is a bridge, a hermeneutical arch that moves the text from its ancient setting to a vibrant, vital word for today.

An *evangelistic objective* is pinpointed if the interpreter determines that the intent of the text is to lead people to find Jesus as their Lord and Savior. John 3:1–21 is such a text.

The *Christian life objective* has four subdivisions:

Consecrative: To lead Christians to perform some Christian service or action, such as witnessing, improving stewardship, or adapting a spirit of submissiveness to God;

Ethical: To improve relationships with others, such as in community race relations or within families;

Doctrinal: To help Christians understand specific doctrines, such as the deity of Christ;

Supportive: To encourage Christians when they have suffered loss or other trauma.

For each biblical text to be interpreted, the preacher must decide if the text is evangelistic or if the text relates to the Christian life, and then to which subdivision of the Christian life.

4. A *Major Objective of the Sermon* (MOS) is a statement of what the preacher hopes to accomplish with this one message, from this one text, for this one congregation, at this one

particular time. This should be a concise, simple sentence. If the MOS is to be related to the Christian life, the MOS can usually be specified in one sentence.

Look at the relationship of the text to all the previously mentioned items. The *CIT* is a direct reflection of the text; the *MOT* is a broad description of the *CIT;* the Thesis is a present-tense application of the CIT. The MOS is determined by the Thesis. Since items two, three, and four are dependent on the CIT, all accordingly reflect the textual content on which the CIT is based.

To write a CIT, especially the first few times, the preacher should seek a unifying theme in the text. For instance, 1 Peter 1:3–12 has the unifying theme of "a living hope." With this concept in mind, the preacher can write a brief summary of the text, relating this précis to the unifying theme. Next the preacher should reduce that summary statement to a simple declarative, past-tense sentence of fifteen to eighteen words, interpreting what the text meant at the time it was written.

Writing the CIT may be the most difficult of these interpretive exercises, but once the CIT is written (even if it is only tentative), the other interpretive items fall easily into place. Although the interpreter must expect to meditate on, wrestle with, write, then rewrite, to arrive at a viable CIT, this grappling with the text is invaluable for sermon preparation. As the central idea is shaped, secondary and marginal ideas implied in the text are seen as such and unrelated ideas are discarded. Writing a CIT puts the interpreter in touch with the "heartbeat" of the text, thereby serving to give direction to the actual sermon preparation. The title, outline, conclusion, introduction, and invitation can usually be evaluated in light of the CIT, which is a direct reflection of the text. By using the CIT, MOT, Thesis, MOS method, the preacher provides maximum assurance that his or her sermon will have a strong relationship to its text. (See Appendix C for a sample CIT, MOT, Thesis, and MOS.)

This process may seem time-consuming at first, but there

are compensations. Each time you use this method it will take less time. You will learn how to consult commentaries and how to locate quickly the information that will be helpful to the interpretive process. You will also be constantly accumulating biblical knowledge, and the more knowledge you have of the Bible, the less time you need to spend in research and study.

Forming the Structure 4

A sermon consists of a title, introduction, body, conclusion, and possibly an invitation. (Some people do not feel an invitation is appropriate or even theologically justified.) Each of these parts of the sermon must be closely related and, as we have already seen, they are strongly related to a biblical text. The title summarizes and gives direction to the sermon. The introduction should draw attention to the theme or subject of the sermon. The body of the sermon develops and expands the theme or subject of the sermon. The conclusion summarizes and often applies the sermon to the congregation. The invitation gives opportunity for the congregation to respond to the sermon in an act of commitment. Obviously, each part of the sermon must be strongly related to the other parts, and all of the parts must be strongly related to the text. A lack of unity or clarity in one or more parts of the sermon would cause the sermon to be vague and confusing to those who hear the sermon.

Preparing Titles

The title for a sermon should be developed as soon as possible during the sermon preparation stages since it will serve as a summary and give direction to the sermon. The title is developed from the subject or theme of the sermon, which should already have been suggested by the CIT, Thesis, MOT and MOS. The title should be clearly phrased and specific, and should avoid vague generalities.

Although the title should be *brief*, using a one-word title is usually too general and contrived. On the other hand, more than seven words produces a cumbersome title. Usually no more than two to seven words is sufficient to indicate the direction of the sermon.

The title should be *creative*. Phrasing it in a fresh, scintillating way, perhaps as a question, increases curiosity and provokes thinking. Consult a thesaurus to locate new words to replace cliches, trite phrases and hackneyed expressions. Always remember, however, to keep in mind the educational and interest level of the prospective audience.

The title should be phrased in *good taste*. Though good taste is difficult to define, avoid profanity, vulgarity, double entendres, or any phrasing that seems questionable. Such titles gain attention, but not the right kind.

Sermon titles may be written in many different ways. For example, an effective title may be one that *emphasizes a key word.*

Title: The *Virtue* of Compassion[1]

Text: Job 16:4 "I also could speak as ye do: if your soul were in my soul's stead."

Another approach to writing a title is the use of an *imperative* statement. The imperative statement emphasizes the verb.

Title: Keep America Christian![2]

Text: Lamentations 5:21 "Turn us unto thee, O Lord, and we shall be turned; renew our days as of old!"

The *interrogative* title can also be an effective approach.

Title: But When Life Tumbles In, What Then?[3]

Text: Jeremiah 12:5 "If thou hast run with the footmen and they have wearied thee, then how canst thou contend with the horses?"

Often, the title may be a simple *declaration.*

Title: Problems Are Good For You[4]

Text: Job 5:7 "Yet man is born unto trouble, as the sparks fly upward."

Most titles *narrow* or *specify* the subject.

Title: The Answer to a Perplexing Question[5]

Text: Matthew 17:19 "Why could we not cast him out?" (KJV)

Preparing the Introduction

A sermon introduction typically has three purposes:

It introduces the biblical text. Sometimes, the text may be read earlier in the worship service. Most often, however, the passage is introduced and read in the opening sentences of the sermon.

It introduces the theme or subject of the sermon. This may be accomplished by stating the title of the sermon. However it is done, the congregation should be told the theme of the sermon somewhere in the introduction.

It establishes relevant contact with the congregation. Meaningful rapport with the congregation is established by telling how or why they need the sermon either as an ongoing principle in their lives or to tie in with a particular event or contemporary problem in their lives.

There are numerous types of introductions. Seven prominent types will be mentioned here for purposes of analysis, but a combination of any or all can be used within a single introduction.

1. Textual—emphasizing the text by reading it, describing its context, historical background, central idea, and thesis (see chapter 3 "Interpreting the Text").

2. Illustrative—using one or more illustrations to convey the text and main theme of the sermon.

3. Title—elaborating on the title and its relation to the text and theme.

4. Application—stating how the text and sermon relate to the congregation and perhaps delineating appropriate responses by the congregation even before the sermon is preached.

5. Striking Quotation—usually used in the first sentence of the sermon to deepen interest in what will come.

6. Rhetorical Questions—deepening congregational interest by one or more probing but rhetorical questions.

7. Object lesson or visual aid—focusing congregational attention on something tangible that can be a means for conveying the theme of the sermon.

Many preachers prefer to prepare the introduction after the title, body, conclusion, and invitation have been completed. Actually, it makes a lot of sense to prepare the introduction last. Only after a given sermon's body and concluding statements are clarified in the preacher's own mind can he or she really know what is being introduced and how to go about it.

Whenever the introduction is prepared, it is worth remembering that a strong introduction is essential to effective preaching. Perhaps the one time in the entire sermon at which most, if not all, the congregation will be listening attentively is during the opening statement. The first few sentences, then, should have strong relevance to the sermon, to the entire context of the worship experience, and to the conclusion and invitation yet to come.

Notice how F. W. Robertson in his sermon "Elijah"[6] uses biblical illustrations to involve his hearers in the sermon and to introduce the subject of the sermon:

Elijah

1 Kings 19:4—"But he himself went a day's journey into the wilderness, and came and sat down under a juniper-tree: and he requested for himself that he might die; and said, It is enough: now, O Lord, take away my life: for I am not better than my fathers."

It has been observed of the holy men of Scripture, that their most signal failures took place in those points of character for which they were remarkable in excellence. Moses was the meekest of men—but it was Moses who "spake unadvisedly with his lips." St. John was the apostle of charity; yet he is the very type to us of religious intolerance, in his desire to call down fire from heaven. St. Peter is proverbially the apostle of impetuous intrepidity: yet twice he is proved a craven. If there were anything for which Elijah is remarkable, we should say it was superiority to human weakness. Like the Baptist he dared to arraign and rebuke his sovereign: like the commander who cuts down the bridge behind him, leaving himself no alternative but death or victory, he taunted his adversaries, the priests of Baal on Mount Carmel. . . . Now it was this man—so stern, so iron, so independent, so above all human weakness, of whom it was recorded that in his trial hour he gave way to a fit of petulance and querulous despondency to which there is scarcely found a parallel. Religious despondency, therefore, is our subject.

Preparing the Body of the Sermon

For many years most preachers prepared the body of their sermons in outline form only. In recent years, however, many preachers have abandoned this slavish devotion to sermon outlines as the *only* way to preach a sermon. The sermon outline, although not as popular as it once was, is still a convenient way to prepare the body of a sermon. Therefore, we will discuss the use of an outline here. In chapter 7, "Varying the Content," we will discuss various other ways of developing the body of a sermon.

An outline gives the sermon a framework which the preacher may develop around a central theme. This framework helps the preacher amplify his or her thoughts in an orderly manner, thus facilitating the congregation's understanding of the text and its relevance.

Some general rules for sermon outlines include:

1. The outline should have a strong, clear relationship to

the title (and thus to the CIT, MOT, Thesis, and MOS as discussed in chapter three).

2. Each major point should discuss only one aspect of the title or theme. Each major point should be distinct from other points. The points should not overlap.

3. Each major point should be written as a complete sentence.

4. Each major point should be written in the present tense so as to apply to today.

5. Each major point should have approximately equal value in the development of the outline.

6. The points should be organized in whatever order and style (e.g. "logical," "poetic," etc.) will best communicate the textual interpretation to a contemporary congregation.

7. The outline should contain specific rather than general wording.

8. Each major point should have a textual basis.

The number of points in an outline depends primarily on how many divisions are in the biblical text. A sermon outline may have two or more points, although a sermon outline with more than four points may be increasingly cumbersome for a congregation to follow.

Notice the unity between the following outline and its text and title:

> Text: Matthew 1:21 ". . . and thou shalt call his name Jesus: for he shall save his people from their sins."
>
> Title: "The Saviourhood of Jesus Christ"[7]
>
> Outline:

> I. The Savior Is Identified ("Thou shalt call his name Jesus")
>
> II. The Savior Is Specified ("He shall save")
>
> III. The Salvation Is Classified ("He shall save his people from their sins")

Preparing the Conclusion

Concluding statements also should always be well prepared. In every form of communication it is recognized that the final impressions the listeners receive will be the ones to which they will respond. Broadus wrote:

> The great orators of Greece and Rome paid much attention to their perorations, seeming to feel that this was the final struggle which must decide the conflict.
> Let us lay down the rule, then, that the conclusion. . . should be carefully prepared.[8]

Sermon conclusions usually contain one or more of the following elements:

1. *Summary or recapitulation.* A review of the sermon can be helpful to the congregation. This review should reinforce in the hearers' minds the most important points of the sermon.

2. *Illustration.* A practical example is often used to help the congregation both to perceive the main idea of the sermon and to empathize with that idea.

3. *Application.* A statement of general applicability to show the congregation how the sermon has meaning for their lives.

Conclusions should accomplish three things:

The conclusion should conclude. This is the time for finalizing or wrapping up the sermon. This is not a time to introduce new ideas. A sense of promise is instilled in the congregation when the preacher says, "In conclusion . . ." or "Finally . . ." or "I close with these words. . . ." The congregation will feel disappointed and perhaps react negatively to the preacher as well as the sermon if this promise is not kept.

The conclusion should be personally meaningful to the congregation. This is a good time to emphasize how the sermon can help the congregation commit their lives in some way, deal with a problem in their lives, challenge them to change an attitude or action, etc. This is a good time to use personal pronouns such as we, us, or you.

The conclusion should make a transition to the invitation. The conclusion specifies how the sermon relates to the congregation, whereas the invitation specifies how and when a response to the sermon should be made.

The conclusion to the sermon "To Whom Shall We Go?"[9] is

an example of a conclusion that first summarizes the sermon's concluding statements in the first two paragraphs; then moves to application in the third paragraph; and then issues a challenge which could be used as a transition to an invitation. The text of the sermon was from John 6:66–69.

All those things I have just been hypothetically describing as the things that we desperately need—the love of God to sinful men, the redemption of the world, the forgiveness of sins, the opportunity of new beginnings, the Kingdom of God, which calls us to its service among our fellows, and which is invincible and everlasting—all that pattern of belief and life is not simply *any* religion or *every* religion: it is the religion of Christ, the Gospel of Christ.

And to crown it all: if the Gospel is true, then not only is the ideal an eternal reality in heaven, not only is the dream an invincible purpose of God, but also: the Word became flesh and dwelt among us on earth: God Himself was incarnate in Jesus Christ and bore the sin of the world for our salvation.

If the Gospel is true, I said. I haven't proved it to be true. I haven't even tried to do that. I don't think anybody can exactly prove it, in black and white on paper. This conviction comes in a different way, when in practice you face up to it. But isn't it something to face up to? It isn't irrelevant. It matters immensely. It is worth believing in. What would life be without a high purpose? What would a high purpose be without religion? And what would religion be without Christ? To whom can we go but unto Him?

That is the Christian inheritance about which you have to make up your mind.

Preparing the Invitation

The theological use of the word *invitation* is not far removed from its everyday use. An invitation extended at the end of a sermon encourages the listeners to make a positive public response to the sermon. An invitation can be beneficial to the congregation as Roy Fish explains:

> These benefits are numerous; they include forgiveness of sin, a new quality of life, peace, purpose, life everlasting. . . . The word "invitation," however, is more encompassing than this. It actually includes any kind of appeal to repent and affirmatively respond to Jesus Christ . . . generally the invitation will include specifying some external form of response to the gospel.[10]

The invitation is the most critical time of the entire worship service, since the responses made during this period will have eternal impact. Such an awesome moment surely deserves the finest preparation, including attention to the following:

1. Extend the invitation *expectantly*. Expect several persons to make a positive response. This sense of expectancy is more than superficial optimism. It reflects one's faith that the Holy Spirit is surely at work in the lives of many members of the congregation.

2. Extend the invitation *clearly*. Specifically tell the congregation *why* they should respond, *how* they should respond, and *when* they should respond. Have you ever noticed the specific instructions Billy Graham gives to his listeners? He usually says, "Right now, I want you to get up out of your chair. I want you to make your way to the front of this platform. I want you to come forward to accept Jesus as your personal Savior." Any preacher's invitation should be as clear and explicit as that.

3. Extend the invitation *authoritatively*. Since the invitation is given by authority of the Word of God, it needs no explanation or apology.

4. Extend the invitation *urgently*. Seek a positive response that will happen now, not later. The very issues involved in the invitation and the various responses possible are intrinsically urgent. To accept Jesus as Lord and Savior, to rededicate one's life to Christ, to respond to a divine vocational

calling, and/or to move the entire membership toward a particular goal are all urgent decisions invited by means of a call at the sermon's end.

Related to the matter of urgency is the manipulation of emotions that is often a valuable preaching technique. Emotions are part of the makeup of every human being, so we need not apologize for an *honest* appeal to them. On the other hand, exploitive emotionalism—that is, the deliberate attempt to manipulate someone into a response that involves only the sensationalism of the moment—should always be avoided in the invitation.

Applying the Dynamics of Self-Expression

5

The sermon must be clearly expressed! This is accomplished by close attention to verbal style, and by an understanding of the functional elements of preaching. Clear verbal style involves the rules of grammar and suggestions as to how verbal style may become more dynamic and appealing. The functional elements of preaching—as its name implies—helps language *function* in the sermon. Without the functional elements of preaching, the language of the sermon could be rambling and confused. The functional elements of preaching uses language in a distinct way to achieve the purpose or objective of the sermons.

Developing Verbal Style

1. *Prepare in an oral rather than written style.* Oral style is less formal and more listener-friendly. It allows for the use of contractions and permits a sentence to start with "And" or "But" as in a conversation.

2. *Try to limit sentences to a maximum of twenty words.* Most listeners lose the train of thought when sentences are longer and complicated by an assortment of modifying clauses.

3. *Get immediately to the point.* Often this means opening the sentence with the subject and following immediately with the verb. Instead of saying, "Among the Minor Prophets is found the book of Amos, from which chapter 3 verse 7, our text for today's sermon, is taken," say, "The text for today's sermon is Amos 3:7."

4. *Pay careful attention to word order.* Be certain that related items in a sentence are positioned together. For example, the following ad, which appeared in a church newsletter, exemplifies the need for proper placement of a modifying phrase: "For Sale: Small Chairs for Children with Straw Seats."

5. *Use the transitive (or active) form of a verb.* Instead of saying, "My conversion experience will always be remembered by me," say, "I will always remember my conversion experience."

6. *Keep adjectives in a minor role.* Remember, that adjectives, though useful, are subjective. Do not overuse them.

7. *Whenever possible, replace the pronouns "it" and "this" with specific nouns.* For example, say "The Bible is a fascinating book," rather than "It is a fascinating book." To avoid excessive repetition of the same antecedent, consult a thesaurus to find suitable synonyms.

8. *Use a topic sentence to begin a new paragraph.* A topic sentence gives an overview of the paragraph it introduces and can preserve listener interest in the general theme of the sermon.

9. *Be a keen student of words.* A rich vocabulary is a preacher's most basic tool, but when words are not used correctly, a sermon's effectiveness is reduced. For example, there is a difference in meaning between the words *anxious* and *eager;* yet preachers often say one when they mean the other.

An interesting exercise in the study of communication is to read the sayings of Jesus. Note that he communicated in simple words and thought forms and made use of straightforward word pictures and analogies. Yet he spoke more profoundly than anyone before or since.

Using the Functional Elements of Preaching

To give purpose and direction to content, a skillful preacher selectively utilizes three functional devices of preaching: *explanation*, *application*, and *argumentation*. Another dynamic, *illustration*, is a "servant" of both explanation and application but will be discussed separately.

Explanation

Broadly defined, *explanation* is a process that makes something clear, or plain, therefore more understandable. The use of explanation in a sermon is almost totally directed to the underlying biblical text, although the technique can be used with reference to nonbiblical data as well. Explaining the text is one of the primary functions of preaching. For this reason, great emphasis has already been placed in this book on spiritual preparation, background study, and interpretation of the text when formulating the CIT, Thesis, and Objectives (*MOT* and *MOS*) of the text. Explanation "opens" the Scriptures—just as Paul did at Thessalonica (Acts 17:3)—and feeds people from the Word. To neglect the use of explanation in a sermon is to withhold the spiritual nourishment of the Word.

Individual words within the passages may need explanation. For example, in 1 Peter 1:4 (e.g., NKJV) the words "inheritance," "incorruptible," "undefiled," and "reserved" may each need to be clearly defined. The lexical resources used in interpretation help us here. "Inheritance" means something handed down or willed to another with such certainty that the inheritor may actually feel a sense of possession. "Incorruptible" means secure from decay. "Undefiled" means free from impurity. "Reserved" means set aside for a special purpose. One or more of these word studies could play a role in developing an overall explanation of the passage.

The *context* of a text may also need to be explained. For example, 1 Peter 1:4 is appositional to the "living hope" mentioned in the previous verse. "Apposition" refers to adjacent placement, for the purpose of building on what is already stated. Verse 4, then, explains or expands what is meant by "living hope" in verse 3. The intrinsic connection between these two verses may have to be explained somewhere in a sermon that uses the biblical text 1 Peter 1:3–12.

An entire biblical *phrase, sentence,* or *verse* may need to be explained. For example, although 1 Peter 1:5 probably would not need a detailed word study, an explanatory summary of the verse might be in order. Such an explanation might include the observation that not only is the "inheritance" (v. 4) secure, but the inheritor is also, in the sense that the inheritor is as closely guarded and protected as the inheritance. Or, to simplify, a Christian is as closely guarded and protected as is the "living hope" that God has granted to all Christians.

Doctrines, too, may need an explanation. We note that 1 Peter 1:3–12 has much to say about salvation, as well as the nature of God and of the Christian life. These are basic doctrines that deserve elaboration.

Finally, it may be helpful to explain the *historical setting* of the text, especially if it clarifies the purpose for writing the passage (or biblical book) under consideration. Thus, studying the background of the 1 Peter 3–12 text indicates that Peter wrote to scattered groups of Christians to encourage them in a time of persecution. His method was to describe the Christian life as the superior way. An understanding of this historical background may be necessary if one is to appreciate the urgency and depth of the entire passage. Far from being just a simple statement of the niceties of salvation, this text was written with a pressing urgency to people who were bewildered by the persecution they were suffering. Explaining the historical setting gives the congregation a proper perspective.

How should the explanation be achieved? Thus far we have discussed some important aspects of the text that may need clarification in the sermon. We next will set forth the various ways this explanatory process may be accomplished.

Exposition is the most common way of doing explanation in a sermon. Exposition reveals information drawn from the background material and the exegetical study. Specifically, exposition may incorporate data from a study of the purpose or occasion for writing a biblical book and/or from a lexical or grammatical study of a particular text. (This has already been illustrated in the preceding section.) As described by H. C. Brown, Jr.:

> Exposition presents truth, facts, and data of all types. More-over, exposition makes assertions, sets out the fruit or results of exegetical work concerning words, phrases, clauses, sentences, and paragraphs from the text.[1]

Another way to present an explanation is by framing a *theological statement* in the form of a conclusion or an *assertion*. Theological statements are built on exposition, but go far beyond that since they represent another step in interpretation. For example, from 1 Peter 1:3–5 might be derived: "The salvation of every Christian is eternal. Once a person is saved, that person is forever saved." This preaching technique achieves "explanation" by revealing doctrinal truth in a statement of a summary and conclusive nature.

A third major explanatory device is *division of the text*, which requires separating the biblical material into two or more points. This type of explanation is used with a rhetorically structured sermon. The very division of the text could be a way to a clearer understanding of the CIT.

Narration (or story-telling) is not only an increasingly popular way of explaining a text but is also the oldest form of communication and is used often in the Bible. Narration draws on setting, characters, and action and thus can have vast appeal to the imagination and emotions of the audience.

Explanation may also be accomplished by *cross references* from Scripture. Identifying a supporting or parallel passage

for the sermon's textual base undergirds the theological statement being made about the text or a portion thereof. For example, John 10:27–30 could be a cross reference for the
theological statement in 1 Peter 1:3–5 about the security of
the Christian's salvation.

Comparison is often cited as another method of explaining
the text. Along with analogy, this technique will be discussed
in the section on illustration.

Explanation is a primary requirement for most preaching,
especially as it feeds people directly from the Word. A sermon's
explanatory elements should not sound as if the preacher were
reading from a biblical commentary. Explanations should be
presented in a clear, forceful, and appealing style. Their purpose is to enhance understanding of portions of the text, but
not necessarily to cover every detail of that text.

The following excerpt demonstrates explanation-by-expo-
sition. The passage is taken from the introduction to a sermon
by Wayne Ward. The text is Mark 1:1–3, 14–15, and the title
of the sermon is "The Gospel of Jesus Christ."

> One of the most beautiful words in the English language is
> the word "gospel." It comes from an Anglo-Saxon root which
> means "God's story" and serves as a very effective translation
> of the New Testament word for good news—the good news of
> the saving work of God which culminated in the cross and
> resurrection of Christ. From the Greek word for gospel we get
> the words "evangel" and "evangelist," terms which denote the
> thrilling story of God's redemptive love, in which He took upon
> himself our humanity and bore our sins on Calvary's cross.
> Many Christians refer to themselves as "evangelicals," because
> they consider it their highest calling to proclaim to a lost world
> the good news of salvation in Jesus Christ.[2]

Notice how the paragraph expounds upon and increases
understanding of the text. Ward shares the information in an
appealing, non-pedantic manner, which is the best way to use
the functional element of explanation in a sermon.

Application

A second functional element found in preaching is *application*, which relates the text to the congregation in such a way that the hearers become involved and helps the congregation to see how the text has meaning for contemporary life. This preaching dynamic might indicate how specific problems can be solved or might challenge individual Christians to grow spiritually. It might show how to perform Christian service, how to live a better life, or how to please God. The methods of application are as varied as people's needs. Whereas explanation focuses on relating the text to the sermon, the aim of application is to make that text relevant to the congregation. Explanation is largely dependent on the CIT, but application is attentive to both the Thesis and the MOS (see chapter 3). Application makes the critical move from the "then" of Scripture to the "here and now" of today:

> A double bridge must be built and crossed by the preacher before he can use application with telling effect. The preacher must move his audience from the Biblical world to the modern world. He must also move his audience from the act of listening to a speaker to an act of personal participation with the preacher as he witnesses to God's self-disclosure in Jesus Christ. When these two bridges are successfully crossed, effective communication takes place between preacher and people.[3]

Effective application uses first- and second-person plural pronouns—"we," "us," "you"—thus making the references strong, personal, and direct. The first person singular ("I," "me," "my,") may be used in special situations, but in general is too limited to be very effective. Third-person pronouns ("he," "she," "they") refer to people who are not in the congregation and are therefore rather weak and impersonal. The preacher must decide when it is best to use a particular pronoun ("*We* should grow in grace!" and/or "*You*, too, can become a child of God!"). The use of "we" establishes a strong rapport with the congregation. When "you" is the form of address, it should never be done in a condescending or arrogant way.

Notice the use of personal pronouns in one paragraph of Harry Emerson Fosdick's sermon "The Power to See It Through:"[4]

> I suspect that this is the outstanding challenge to us in the churches—our attitude not on theological questions but on practical, ethical, social questions. We find it easy to love this present age. We make fine beginnings, especially at New Year's time, but then some comfortable corner of this present age invites us and we nestle down. So our Christian profession lapses, our faith grows formal, and we do not amount to much in the end as Christians. If I should accuse some of you of being Judas Iscariot you would be indignant. You would never deliberately sell anybody out. But Demas—ah, my soul, how many of us have been that!

Occasionally, application can be made in the third person (e.g., "the person who lies," "the taxpayer who cheats"). On those occasions the preacher may feel that an indirect approach is superior to a direct approach.

Application may deal with what in the text is relevant to the congregation and why, when, and how this is so. The preacher may also want to address the possible results of adopting (or not adopting) the applicable portions of the text. It may be enough to point out that the text *does* relate to a congregation, but many congregations lack the theological, hermeneutical, and spiritual skills to determine the specifics of application for themselves. In cases where the audience appears to be weak in the resolve and desire to make self-application, the preacher may employ "exhortation," which has an undeservedly bad reputation in some circles. Exhortation simply means a strong and sincere plea from the preacher to the congregation to respond to the implied commands of the text.

Argumentation

The goal of *argumentation* is to persuade someone to change an attitude or an action. This functional element of preaching is not used today as often or as artfully as it was prior to this century. John Calvin and Charles Finney, to name just two, were preachers who used argumentation effectively. It is significant that both men received training in the law before they became preachers, although the apostle Paul also used this technique competently and yet had no specific legal training. The use of argumentation calls for a strong sense of discernment—the ability to identify issues and discuss them logically.

Argumentation from Testimony

This form of argumentation cites a person or persons whose opinions or findings would be considered authoritative. Such information is intended to add credibility to the position taken by the preacher. For example, if Billy Graham, Harry Emerson Fosdick, or Albert Schweitzer is cited on a theological or social issue, many persons will feel that such testimony would advance the sermon's overall objective.

Argument by Refutation

Here is a form of argumentation that calls for tact and diplomacy. To "refute" means to prove to be erroneous or false. Since, in preaching, argumentation is supposed to persuade someone to receive the gospel or to change an attitude or action, it is advisable to use refutation only in a way that will not cause counterattacks or negative feelings.

Reproval and *rebuke* are a step behind refutation, but—when used argumentatively—they warrant the same cautions. To "reprove" is to express disapproval, and to "rebuke" is to censure or scold sternly with a view to setting things in order. Similarly, to "reprimand" is to offer a strong, formal criticism, usually by a person in authority. While not as strong as refutation, a reproof, rebuke, or reprimand can serve the same purpose: "winning" a discussion.

There are perhaps situations in which refutation is the best way to employ argumentation in a sermon. Jesus used refutation, for example, against the Pharisees in Matthew 23.

Argument by Inference

A third type of argumentation is *inference*, which uses inductive, deductive, or analogical approaches to lead people to a particular decision.

The *inductive* approach moves from particular data or experiences to a generalization or conclusion. This approach is especially useful in exploring biblical and extra-biblical data with the congregation and then arriving at a conclusion (or hypothesis) together. Ideally, an inductive approach allows the evidence to draw the listeners to a conclusion of their own.

The *deductive* approach begins with a basic premise (or hypothesis) and then brings evidence to support that premise. Most preaching is done this way, one advantage being that so many people have been conditioned to think deductively. The chief disadvantage to this approach is that often the conclusion and so-called evidence are presented with extreme bias.

The *analogical* approach, which uses comparison and contrast, may be the single most effective method of argumentation. An analogy states or implies similarities between two or more concepts, the aim being to advance a particular premise or argument based on those likenesses. Several studies have indicated that a change of attitude or action is much more likely to occur as a result of argumentation that includes analogy than with an approach that does not.[5]

Argument by Specialized Forms

Six specialized forms of argumentation will be defined and illustrated here.

A priori reasons from cause to effect. An example is Paul's statement: "Therefore, since we have been justified through faith [cause], we have peace with God [effect] through our Lord Jesus Christ" (Rom. 5:1).

A posteriori reasons from effect back to cause. Common sense must conclude that a watch with its intricate functions requires one who designed and made it. Similarly, our solar system and universe with the precise movements of planets and stars indicate a designer and maker—God the creator.

A fertiori reasons from a weaker example to a strong one. Jesus used this effectively in pointing out that if humans, who are sinful, can give good gifts to their children [weak example], "how much more will your Father in heaven [strong example] give good gifts to those who ask him!" (Matt. 7:11).

Ex concesso reasons from that which has been conceded. When Paul at Athens addressed pagan philosophers, he led them to easily concede—through their own altar to "an unknown God"—that they were open to more information about God, which Paul then readily shared.

Reductio ad absurdum reduces the matter being argued to the absurd. Some people in the Corinthian church contended that there is no resurrection of the dead. Paul countered: "For if the dead are not raised, then Christ has not been raised either. And if Christ has not been raised, your faith is futile; you are still in your sins" (1 Cor. 15:16, 17). In comparing this contention to the reality of Christ's resurrection, the argument of these Corinthians became absurd.

Ad hominem appeals to personal interests, prejudices, or emotions rather than to reason. The prophet Nathan used a simple story (cf. 2 Sam. 12) that evoked a strong emotional response from David. The rich man (owner of many sheep), who demanded the one lamb that belonged to a poor man, ". . . deserves to die" exclaimed David, burning with anger. Nathan said to David, "You are the man." David immediately saw his guilt in striking down Uriah to make his marriage to Bethsheba appear legitimate. (Even though the technical names of these forms sound a little forbidding, these types of argument are not uncommon in sermons.)

The following excerpt, an example of argument by refutation, is from a sermon by Millard Berquist. The title of the sermon is: "America's #1 Health Problem—Alcoholism."

> Who is it that champions the cause of moderation? It's the unthinking man or woman who selfishly and self-righteously says, "It's no problem to me. I can take it or leave it. I know when to stop. I have learned to control my drinking"; this person shows no semblance of deep social concern for the youth of America or for the survival of America. Who else champions the cause of moderation? The brewers, the distillers, and the liquor dealers who are not concerned about excess but who use "moderation" as a sales gimmick to enhance the sale of their deceptive and destructive product and who sneer at Jesus Christ who said, "What shall it profit a man, if he shall gain the whole world, and lose his own soul?" Moderation is foreign to alcohol. It is no joke to me to hear of high school sons and daughters of moderationist parents, who joke about staying up past midnight to see if mother and dad are able to navigate when they get home at two in the morning. . . . [6]

Illustration

Illustration serves either explanation or application, and is therefore not considered a separate functional element of preaching. Its verb form, "illustrate," comes from the Latin *illustrare*, which means "to cast light upon." A sermon illustration has a specific, narrowly assigned, and limited role: to cast light on one or more facets of an explanation or application.

It is interesting to note that the nature and importance of an illustration are much more far-reaching than its role definition suggests. Since the most remembered portions of most sermons by most congregations will usually be the illustrations, they must be strongly related to the explanation or application they are meant to illuminate. Note, then, the paradox that an illustration, by its very nature, often outshines the material to which it refers. Illustrations must therefore be chosen carefully so as to fulfill their "servant" role without diminishing explanation and application.

Sources of Illustrations

Where are illustrations to be found? The answer is "everywhere," a response that is not intended to be facetious. The real question is: Where may I find the particular illustration needed for a particular place in a particular sermon? That specific question, unfortunately, can be answered only in a general way. Check with a local bookstore for suggestions on sermon illustration sourcebooks. Often these books will have information on various filing systems which may be adapted to your personal preference.

Each preacher must develop an individual filing system that will allow for locating specific illustrations when they are needed. To build a backlog of illustrative material, the preacher must become sensitive to a multitude of potential illustrations.

Current events provide one readily available source of such material. For example, a recent newspaper article mentioned that families of certain airplane crash victims would be awarded $500,000 each. One preacher, sensitive to the article's potential, used it as an illustration in a sermon entitled "How Much Is a Life Worth?" The text was John 3:16.

Other sources of illustrative material include:

1. The Bible (especially its stories about people)
2. Autobiographies and biographies
3. History books
4. Hymnology
5. Literature (both poetry and prose)
6. Science (all branches: e.g., biology, chemistry, math, physics, astronomy, mathematics)
7. Sports accounts (especially useful in discussing "discipline")
8. The arts (painting, sculpture, music and dance, drama)

Types of illustrations

Sermon illustrations appear in two broad literary styles: anecdotes and figurative speech.

Anecdotes are short narratives about some interesting character or situation. They are often humorous (but not necessarily so) and place an emphasis on the personalities involved and other human-interest elements. Story-telling has always been an immensely popular form of communication. When not overused, a simple story that casts light on either explanation or application is a highly effective method of conveying truth and thus can serve preaching very well.

Personal anecdotes can be a powerful form of sermon illustration and are therefore quite popular with preachers. Care must be taken, however, not to overuse them in the pulpit, even if they are applied with integrity. Although congregations can usually empathize with a preacher's first-person stories, they can also become weary of hearing too much "I," "me," and "my" in a sermon.

There are several types of *figurative speech* that can be used effectively as illustrative material in a sermon:

A *simile* is an explicit comparison of two basically unlike objects and is usually identified by the use of the words *like* or *as.* For example, "Pharaoh's heart was cold as a witch's kiss."

A *metaphor* is a comparison that is drawn by identifying one object with another and thus implying their similarity. Jesus did this, for example, in the Sermon on the Mount, when he said, "you are the salt of the earth . . . you are the light of the world . . ." (Matt. 5:13a, 14a).

An *analogy* is an inference that if two (or more) things agree with one another in some respects, they will probably be alike in others. Analogy can explain the unfamiliar in terms of the familiar. For example, the apostle Paul used the one-body/many-parts analogy to explain believers' relationship to the church (and each other).

Hyperbole is a figure of speech that uses excessive exaggeration to make a point. It is usually a deliberate overstatement, such as "a thousand thanks," or a fanciful claim, such as being "tired to death." On the other hand, a *litote* is a deliberate understatement that is often employed for the sake of humor, as in: "It is not particularly appetizing to find a moving object in one's soup."

Euphemisms are words used to soften a term that may be considered harsh, blunt, or indelicate. For example, death is often referred to as "passing away."

Oxymoron uses a combination of words that sound contradictory or incongruous, such as, "Preaching is a rich poverty," or "Honesty can be a cruel kindness."

Catachresis changes one word for another only remotely associated with it, and the association is often incongruous. For example, Hosea 14:2 ". . . so that we may present our lips as bulls" (see NIV marginal note).

Synecdoche is a figure of speech that uses the part for a whole, or the whole for a part, as in Psalm 50:10: ". . . the cattle upon a thousand hills [are mine]."

Metonymy is a figure of speech that uses the name of one person, place, or thing for that of something else with which it is identified. For instance, an alcoholic is said to have a problem with "the bottle."

Billy Graham used a beautiful illustration as the opening paragraph of a sermon titled "The Suffering Saviour on a Crimson Cross." The source of the illustration is from the history of Christian hymnology.

On the south coast of China, on a hill overlooking the harbor of Macao, Portuguese settlers once built a massive cathedral. But a typhoon proved stronger than the work of man's hands. Some centuries ago the building fell in ruins except for the front wall. High on the top of that jutting wall, challenging the elements down through the years, is a great bronze cross. When Sir John Bowring saw it in 1825, he was moved to write those words now so familiar to us all: "In the cross of Christ I glory,

Tow'ring o'er the wrecks of time, All the light of sacred story Gathers round its head sublime." We gather once a year as Christians to consider anew the significance of Jesus' death upon the Cross. Choirs across the world sing, "When I survey the wondrous cross, On which the Prince of glory died, My richest gain I count but loss, And pour contempt on all my pride."[7]

If illustrations are pertinent and tangible to a congregation, they are easily remembered. That is exactly why illustrations need to be used carefully. Be sure that the illustration substantially connects to the explanation or application in relevance and degree. For example, do not compare the emotions raised by an irritating personnel situation in church with what Harry Truman felt when he ordered the atomic bomb dropped on Nagasaki. Conversely, do not compare the decision to dismiss a church staff member to what is involved in choosing between two flavors of ice cream. Remember, the illustration is meant to cast light, not blur the issues.

General Guidelines

There is no set order in which the aforementioned functional elements should be used. A sermon may begin with either (1) explanation, (2) application, (3) argumentation, (4) explanation by illustration, or (5) application by illustration. There should be some balance and proportion in the use of these devices in a sermon. A complicated and detailed explanation may contain more information than the congregation can absorb at one time, or it may make the sermon too didactic. Too much application and too little explanation, on the other hand, will lead to a shallow sermon. Since application builds on explanation, without some explanation of the text there will be nothing to "apply." Similarly, argumentation is meaningless if it is not based on explanation or application or both. Argumentation is not vital to a sermon, but preaching cannot exist without explanation and application.

Finally, as we have seen, illustrations are "servants" and have no reason for existence apart from their support of explanation or application. Although sermons could be preached without them, illustrations are strongly recommended.

Sermons will vary as to the amount of explanation, application, argumentation, or illustration that is required, and as to where each of these functional elements should appear. A specific biblical passage may require more explanation or application at one time than another, depending on the makeup of the congregation, the time of year, or even recent news items. There is no specific rule as to how much of each element should be used in a given sermon. These decisions are based on the preacher's judgment during each sermon's preparation period. Ultimately the effectiveness of the functional elements is dependent on the preacher's ability to use words effectively.

Evaluating the Product ⟩ **6**

Purposeful evaluation of a sermon *before* it is preached can do much for a preacher's confidence and indirectly strengthen his or her communicative skills. This evaluation should cover the biblical authority of the sermon, and the clarity or logical progression of the sermon.

Checking for Biblical Authority

As we have seen, the relationship between a sermon and its text is extremely important. One widely circulated joke in the church centers around the preacher who reads a text, never to return thereto. There is a serious message for us in that bit of humor. (In fact, two important rules that every preacher should remember are (1) quit when you are through and (2) preach on the text you have announced.) A biblical sermon is one that has an obvious and strong relationship to its text. It may include the sharing of editorial, personal, or devotional thoughts only as they shed light or otherwise have bearing on the announced text.

A sermon based on Scripture is controlled or guided by its biblical text, but using a text does not force a set form or approach on the preacher. A biblical sermon can be (and ought to be) creative, fresh, and scintillating within the parameters of the passage on which it based.

There are various kinds of authority. *Imperial authority* is exercised by kings and queens over their subjects. *Delegated authority* has specified limitations and its dimensions are usually stipulated by contracts or by-laws. It is exercised in the church by pastors, committees, superintendents, officers, and teachers, and in secular life by police officers, military officers, or public officials. *Functional authority*, a subdivision of delegated authority, is exercised, for example, by a committee (or subcommittee) chairperson. "Custom" is an important and often unspecified type of functional authority. This is the kind of authority recognized by those who say, "This is the way we have always done it," or words to that effect. Finally, *veracious authority* is based on whatever is perceived as true. Obviously, the Bible serves as veracious authority in the church. Without the abiding and unquestionable truths of the Bible, there would be chaos for preacher and congregation alike. If truth were merely what each individual decided it was, we would be reliving the dark time of the Judges when "every man did that which was right in his own eyes" (Judg. 20:25). The veracious authority of the Bible exists whether or not we accept it.

A sermon may reflect one of three different kinds of biblical authority: *direct, secondary,* or *casual.* Or it may call on a *combination* of these approaches.[1]

Direct Biblical Authority

A direct biblical sermon has the same message or meaning or intent as does its biblical text. This type of preaching uses the historical-grammatical-theological approach to the fullest degree. In effect, the CIT and Thesis govern the development of a direct biblical sermon.

Broadly speaking, the direct biblical sermon seeks to communicate the eternal truths of Scripture. These are found in all the various kinds of literature in the Bible, whether they be historical or biographical narratives, parables, proverbs, poems, psalms, figures of speech, commands (both positive and negative), or affirmations. As we have seen previously, the CIT attempts to see truth in its biblical setting and the Thesis attempts to apply that timeless truth to our time.

To cite a couple of examples, the eternal truths of Psalm 73 broadly involve the problem of evil and suffering and, more specifically, the hope of the righteous in light of the apparent prosperity of the wicked. There are other secondary, related, or marginal sermon ideas in Psalm 73, such as God's infinite love and patience or his inimitable purposes.

To cite another example, Matthew 28:18–20 contains a command. A direct biblical sermon from this text, therefore, would involve discipling, baptizing, and teaching throughout the world.

Picture the direct biblical sermon as a straight arrow moving from the biblical text to the congregation.

Secondary Biblical Authority

A biblical text contains not only direct or primary truths, but also secondary truths, some of which can be developed into viable biblical sermons. When an idea is "secondary" within a text, it is not necessarily insignificant. The secondary idea in a text will often be the very authoritative idea that needs to be preached to a specific congregation at a specific time. In that case it is important to indicate somehow to the congregation that the sermon is dealing with a secondary idea of the text rather than its primary truth.

The secondary truth in a text may be communicated in one of three ways:

1. *Comparison/contrast.* This process sketches a parallel between the biblical text and some other circumstance or situation. The preacher may use physical terms to explain a spiritual truth—or vice versa. Actually, what such a sermon is doing is creating an analogy. This dynamic is different from interpreting an analogy already found in a text or from using one or more analogies as illustrations within a sermon. (Note that interpreting an analogy within a text, if done correctly, could lead to a direct biblical sermon.) Comparing/contrasting biblical truth is illustrated in the well-known sermon "Spiritual Leprosy."[2] This sermon is based on Leviticus 14:1–2: "This shall be the law of the leper for the day of his cleansing . . ." (NKJV)—and it compares the physical disease of leprosy with the spiritual disease of sin. The resulting sermonic analogy effectively preaches important truths about sin, although these truths are secondary to the main thrust of the text.

The preacher must be especially careful not to trivialize Scripture when using the comparison/contrast approach. The sermon on "Spiritual Leprosy" carefully establishes the theme's secondary relationship to the main substance of the text to which it is referenced. However, a sermon from Genesis 6:4a preached on the "giants" of alcoholism, lottery, or any other sin would have no basic parallelism with the text. Nor would a sermon from 1 Samuel 17:49 on slinging the stones of righteousness or justice against the evil "giants" in our land today have even a marginal connection to the biblical truths in that specific passage. Sermons on those topics have biblical texts that can be used more suitably. There is never a good reason for trivializing a text by attempting to force it into a preconceived sermon topic.

2. *Specifying a general truth.* Another way to draw on secondary biblical authority is to specify a broad statement of principle within a sermon. The preacher is here presuming that the biblical author and Christians in general would find agreement with the sermon's specific application. This ap-

proach tends to lend itself to a syllogistic procedure, which involves two premises and a conclusion. It must be carefully used, so that the sermon truly relates substantially to the text.

As an example, note the broadly stated biblical principle in Romans 12:9b: "Hate what is evil . . ." (NIV). Many contemporary problems could be specified under this text, not the least of which are drug abuse, child abuse, and pornography. Although the Bible does not specifically speak on these issues, scriptural authority and Christians in general would have no problem with identifying these and other current issues as evils that should be abhorred.

3. *Validating an implication in Scripture.* This sermonic device presumes that a certain implication exists in the text and is not merely an imaginative creation of the preacher. There are numerous biblical passages that contain implied truths. For example, Exodus 20:7 *implies* that we are to reverence the name of the Lord our God. The command not to "steal" (Exod. 20:15) *implies* that we are to respect the rights of others as to their property or possessions. Similarly, Matthew 5:13 *implies* that we—"the salt of the earth"—are to be active Christian servants in preserving godly principles and arresting the spread of moral decay. Of course, the preacher should do a thorough background study and exegesis to determine whether a given text contains an implication and, if it does, must be able to identify it accurately.

Since the use of secondary biblical authority is potentially confusing to congregations, it is wise to indicate to them that a secondary, or indirect, truth of the text will be preached. This information does not require an apology, but rather a simple explanation. For example, a sermon preached from 1 Peter 1:3–12 would have the primary, or direct, idea of "the living hope." One of the secondary truths might be stated as the joy of our secure salvation (v. 6a). A simple explanation to the congregation might be: "Peter wrote of a living hope. Part of that hope is built on the security of our salvation, and that is the subject of this sermon."

When preparing a sermon that draws on secondary biblical authority, an additional item needs to be added to the preliminary data (see "Theological Resources" in chapter 3). A parenthetical statement should be inserted between the CIT and the Thesis. This statement, which is actually a *secondary CIT,* then dictates the direction of the rest of the preliminary data. When a sermon is built on a secondary truth in the text, why is it even necessary to write a CIT? The answer becomes obvious when we consider that a CIT puts other textual information in sharp focus. Writing a CIT and then adding a secondary idea greatly enhances the accuracy of handling indirect biblical truths.

Preaching from a secondary idea of the text can be pictured this way:

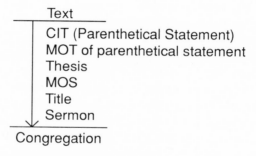

Text

CIT (Parenthetical Statement)
MOT of parenthetical statement
Thesis
MOS
Title
Sermon

Congregation

Casual Biblical Authority

Since a sermon with casual biblical authority has a rather loose relationship to its biblical text, the disadvantages of this approach are obvious. A steady diet of sermons based on vaguely defined biblical authority could leave a congregation spiritually anemic. Casual use of Scripture allows far too much subjectivism. Such a sermon is usually marked by the preacher's oft repeated references to "I," "me," and "my."

The advantages of preaching such a sermon may not be so obvious. A sermon with casual biblical authority can bring a fresh, sparkling approach to a tried-and-true concept. The creative juices of a preacher can find outlet in this approach, but—as always when dealing with Scripture—creativity should never take precedence over accuracy of interpretation.

Unfortunately, many casually drawn sermons have no relation to their announced text. Perhaps the classic example of this failing is the sermon with a specified text of Luke 2:1–11 but whose subject matter covers the advantages of stall feeding as compared to pasture grazing. A casual idea suggested by a passage can be a valid topical option for the preacher only if care is taken to maintain some relation to the announced text.

There are three primary techniques that are effective in developing a sermon with casual biblical authority:

1. *Rhetorical suggestions.* These "suggestions" are inferred from the text. Rhetorical suggestions may seem to have little to do with the central idea of the text (CIT) since they can relate to the text in varying degrees. An example of a sermon using this device and where the suggestion *does* have an apparent relationship to the text is taken from Philippians 4:22: "All the saints salute you, chiefly they that are of Caesar's household." The direct teaching of this text is obvious, though a little mundane: *Fellow Christians send their greetings.* The loosely drawn suggestion is a good one for preaching: *Christians in the most difficult place (Caesar's household) send their greetings.* Thus, a preacher might prepare a sermon on being a Christian in a difficult place and/or at a difficult time.

2. *Spiritual essays.* Occasionally, issues arise that should be addressed in a sermon but for which there seems to be no specific biblical text. Spiritual essays delivered from the pulpit have topics that range from why we should (or should not) build civil-defense shelters and whom we should allow to enter them, whether ballistic missiles should ever be used, whether we should trade with Red China (or South Africa), why Christians should (or should not) be immensely wealthy, and why we should favor certain architectural styles for church buildings.

It is difficult to schematize a sermon with casual biblical authority, as was done for sermons with direct and even secondary authority. Think of the straight line of a direct biblical sermon as a high-powered electrical connection. Every em- powered electric wire has a field of energy emanating from it. You notice this on your car radio, for instance, when you drive beneath power lines: driving through this field of energy causes static to be heard through the speakers. When you have driven out of the energy field, the static disappears. The closer to the power line, the stronger the field of energy; the farther from the power line, the weaker the field of energy. Sermons with casual biblical authority are somewhere within the "field of energy" of the biblical text.

3. *Incidental analogies.* Incidental matters or items in the text often serve as the focal point of sermons. Many sermons developed from the David and Goliath story, for example, have focused on the five smooth stones David selected (1 Samuel 17:40). In such sermons these stones become analogous to the importance of our selection of churches to attend, or which version of the Bible to read, etc. These kinds of sermons are still widely used even though there is little about them that is spiritually uplifting.

Combination Biblical Authority

Any number of combinations of the three types of biblical authority may be used in preaching. A given sermon may in- clude one point built on direct biblical authority and another point built on an implication in the text. Another sermon may reflect direct biblical authority until its conclusion, at which time a general truth may be specified for application to a par- ticular congregation. Using the CIT as a reference point, a preacher should be able to identify when each of the various kinds of biblical authority is used within a sermon.

Checking for Clarity

As important as evaluating the biblical authority of the message may be, lack of clarity can be fatal to a sermon's effectiveness. Measuring the clarity and logical progression of a sermon involves determining the relationship between its various parts: introduction, body, conclusion, invitation. This evaluation takes into account the interconnection of the paragraphs and sentences within each part. It also considers the smoothness of movement of the sermon, which is achieved by the appropriate use of transition sentences.

There are no set rules to guarantee clarity in a sermon, especially since what may be understandable to the preacher may not be as obvious to the congregation. Most preachers, however, are sensitive to their audience and sensible enough to make some preliminary judgments in evaluating the clarity of a sermon's content and pertinence. A convenient method for evaluating clarity is to test each paragraph by asking why that particular paragraph is at that location. This kind of examination helps the preacher see and feel the progressive movement of the sermon. Under such scrutiny it may be apparent that some paragraphs are too personal or subjective and should be removed. For example, bitter diatribe on something that bothers the preacher, but has nothing to do with the rest of the sermon, may need to be eliminated. A paragraph that shares something "cute" that the preacher's children did last week may be amusing, but it should usually be removed if it contributes nothing to the objectives of the sermon or interpretation of the text. Some paragraphs may need elaboration or rearrangement to enhance general clarity. This exercise requires varying degrees of effort and time, but is extremely beneficial to the sermon as a whole. The illustration below consists of sample pages from a sermon by Dr. Bob Ellis.[3] In the left column Dr. Ellis indicates the functional element used in each paragraph (see chapter 5). (*Expl.*—explanation; *Ill.*—illustration; *Appl.*—application.) In the center is the sermon's content. The right column contains a statement of rationale for each paragraph.

Before this sermon was preached, Bob Ellis had thoroughly prepared and evaluated his message. The outcome of this two-step process was, for Ellis, a sense of confidence that he truly had a word from the Lord to the congregation. A natural side effect was that the congregation received with ease a clear, strong word from the Lord. The prospect of such positive results should make every step in sermon preparation a gratifying experience.

Expl.	1. Is justice a figment of God's imagination? The ideal of justice is that good men are rewarded for their righteousness and evil men are punished for their wickedness. But, in practice so often the order seems to be reversed.	*To introduce the problem addressed in Psalm 37*
Expl. by Ill.	Today, evil men get rich through such pursuits as gambling casinos, distilleries, and pornography houses. That neighbor who lied about his income tax can afford a new car this year. The guys who sit on the back row of algebra class cheated on the last test, and they both got A's in the course. On the other hand, good people suffer. The honest bookkeeper at the factory who refused to juggle the books for the company's sake was fired. Christian missionaries are jailed in communist countries. Innocent children are killed in terrorist raids in the Middle East. It seems that the lot of evil men gets	*To illustrate the problem by giving examples.*

better, while the lot of good men gets worse. Does God *really* care about good and evil?

Expl. 2. This preacher is not the first to voice such a question. The problem of recompense and retribution is ageless. Israel, God's chosen people, were one group who struggled with this issue. The Jews looked around themselves, and they saw seeming injustices. They asked the same question which we ask: "Has God forgotten the good people?"

To affirm the existence of the problem for all people.

To relate the problem to the text.

Expl. 3. The question does not go unanswered. The Thirty-seventh Psalm has a bold reply. As the people complained about seeming injustices, the Psalmist replied:
(1) Fret not thyself because of evildoers, neither be thou envious against the workers of iniquity. (2) For they shall soon be cut down like the grass, and wither as the green herb. (3) Trust in the LORD, and do good; so shalt thou dwell in the land, and verily thou shalt be fed.
(4) Delight thyself also in the LORD; and he shall give thee

To introduce the text.

the desires of thine heart.
(5) Commit thy way unto the
LORD; trust also in him; and
he shall bring it to pass.
(6) And he shall bring forth
thy righteousness as the
light, and thy judgment as
the noonday. (7) Rest in the
LORD, and wait patiently for
him: fret not thyself because
of him who prospereth in his
way, because of the man who
bringeth wicked devices to
pass (KJV).

Expl.	4. In verses 1 and 2 we are told that evil men will be "cut down." Any present reward	*To divide the text and intro-duce the CIT.*
Appl.	for them is temporary. They will not escape God's judg-ment; doom awaits them and	*To justify the focus of the sermon.*
Expl.	is not far off. While this neg-ative part of judgment must be kept in mind, there is a positive side which is espe-cially significant for God's people. It is given in verses 3 through 6 and is the focal point of this sermon. The central idea of these five verses is that God promised to reward those who trusted in him.	*To give the CIT.*
Appl.	5. Since the issue of appar-ent injustice is still a nagging question, the psalm-ist's answer is just as	*To state the value of the text for modern man and to*

valuable for us today as it was centuries ago. The words of Scripture break through the years of history to proclaim their message in the twentieth century. The good man need not be confused by seeming inequities around him. God's law is still in effect: he promises to reward whoever trusts in Him.

introduce the Thesis.

Varying the Content 7

Preaching, far more than many other forms of communication, offers numerous possibilities for variety within the boundaries of sound biblical interpretation. By way of contrast, television programs in general, whether they be sit-coms, documentaries, westerns, mysteries—or police, medical, or family dramas—all have rather predictable scenarios. Characters are introduced with sympathy channeled to some and scorn to others. Then a conflict arises with which we are to empathize until a resolution to the conflict provides the happily-ever-after conclusion. For various psychological and commercial reasons, television, movie, and stage dramas are generally confined to this format. But preaching can and should be done with more ingenuity.

Preaching in the Bible is not predictable. The Sermon on the Mount essentially presents a number of biblical and extra-biblical sayings to which Jesus imparted deeper meanings and directly applied those meanings. On the other hand, Peter's sermon at Pentecost, which began with a direct reference to himself, contains quotes from the Old Testament, application with strong exhortation, and an invitation to make a specific response. Jeremiah wore an ox yoke, Isaiah wore the garb of a slave, and Ezekiel used a clay model of a city under siege. Today we would say they used "object lessons" or "visual aids" in their preaching. Amos used a psychological ploy to make a point in his first sermon to Israel.

Throughout the history of preaching, a variety of sermon forms and approaches have been used. The eloquent homilies of Chrysostom are different from the thunderous approach of Luther, which was quite unlike the poetic style of Assisi, which was far removed from Bonhoeffer's courageous stand. Throughout Christian history, preaching has persisted in its basic message, yet adjusted its approach and context according to the personal style of the preacher and to the demands of communicating to a contemporary congregation.

Most preachers and congregations prefer variety. As Spurgeon reminds us:

> Everybody knows what interest there is in fresh work. A gardener will become weary of this toil unless he is allowed to introduce new flowers into the hothouse, or to cut the beds upon the lawn in a novel shape; all monotonous work is unnatural and wearying to the mind, therefore it is wisdom to give variety to your labor.[1]

The more predictable the content and delivery method of a sermon, the more likely it is that the potential for a positive response to the sermon has been diminished. Anyone who has ever visited a ranch has noticed that the narrow path through a pasture usually leads to water. The cows walk the same path to water every day. To find the water, they just step into the rut and follow it. But preachers want to lead people to *living* water, which is rarely found while plodding through a rut. Fortunately, there are several ways to lead congregations to the truth of the living Word of God.

Dramatic Monologues

The dramatic monologue is a popular way of doing innovative preaching, and is similar to the I-was-there-and-now-you-are-there-with-me approach sometimes used in radio or television documentaries. Here the perspective is usually that of a biblical character speaking to the congregation.

A dramatic monologue generates strong congregational interest because people are usually interested in what other people feel and how they react in a given situation. This human-interest quality is one of the main advantages of the monologue format. As important as facts or exegetical data may be to a sermon, they can be too abstract for some people. However, biblical exposition that is related to the life of another person seems to have an immediate attraction.

The preparation of a dramatic monologue calls for some extra effort on the preacher's part. Of course, intense study of the Bible is vital in all preaching, but the dramatic monologue calls for both biblical research and historical research related to the cultural setting of the particular Bible character being portrayed. Resources available for this groundwork include books and articles on the history of biblical times, articles on the selected character in Bible encyclopedias and dictionaries, and exegeses of pertinent biblical material.

The basic organization of the dramatic monologue will be the same as in most sermons—introduction, body, conclusion, and invitation—although the content of the material and style of delivery will be different. For example, although the text may be read at the beginning of the monologue, it more likely will be interspersed throughout the sermon to increase dramatic impact. The introduction should include the theme of the sermon with respect to the biblical character. The preacher may want to speak about the character (in third person) at first or may instead speak *as* the character throughout the sermon.

The body of the sermon may include a first-person narrative tantamount to an "autobiography" of the biblical character being portrayed. Such a narrative will include historical references (for example, "In my day it was customary for the rabbi or the teacher to be seated as he taught") and should be organized around the pertinent biblical materials.

Application of the message is a little more difficult to achieve in a dramatic monologue than in more traditional formats. The application may be the direct here-is-what-you-should-do, or here-is-what-you-should-learn-from-this approach. Or application may take the form of indirect reflective thoughts by the biblical character, from which the congregation is to deduce the application.

The best illustrative material for a dramatic monologue is analogy, although the monologue itself has the impact of a broad analogy. Specific comparisons can be drawn between events in the life of the biblical character and events in the lives of the congregation.

The conclusion of a dramatic monologue is used—as it is in other sermon formats—to summarize, to make additional application to the congregation, and to make a transition to the invitation, which places special emphasis on the objectives of the sermon.

The dramatic monologue, when sincere and done well, usually has a significant impact on the congregation and elicits a strong, positive response. This type of sermon may be delivered in full costume or in contemporary dress. Principles of effective delivery (to be discussed in a later chapter) will apply in full to the dramatic monologue.

Biographical Sermons

Some pastors preach *about* a biblical character without actually role-playing that character. The preparation of a biographical sermon follows the same pattern used for a dramatic monologue; i.e., biblical and historical research. Biographical preaching, as does the dramatic monologue, also has built-in human interest appeal. The primary ways to develop a biographical sermon are:

Life Analysis

This type of preaching highlights certain aspects of the biblical record of a particular Bible character. The Bible varies in the amount and in the kind of information it contains on various persons. The biblical character may be introduced at full maturity (as with Abraham) or at least in adulthood as with Elijah, Peter, or Paul. The lives of others are recorded for us from womb to tomb, as in the case of Jacob, Moses, or Samuel. Life analysis preaching generally portrays the characters' virtues and vices, with a view to convincing the listener to emulate their good qualities and avoid their bad ones. This approach can be only as specific as the biblical details and available time will allow. A study of the entire life of Jacob, for instance, would be too involved for a thorough analysis, while a biographical sermon on Samson could be much more concise.

Very often there are gaps in our information about some biblical characters. In such instances it is permissible to do limited speculation to fill in some of the gaps. Such conjecture must be built only on careful study of the biblical data and the historical setting of the individual being studied. A preacher must be especially careful not to indulge in fanciful hypotheses about a biblical hero and thus distort the biblical record.

Career Analysis

This approach is similar to life analysis except that emphasis is placed on the achievements and shortcomings in the *career* of the biblical character. As we trace the kingship of David, for instance, we discover both his dedication to God and his human frailties. The career of Peter can also be divided into two levels of performance. With apologies to Charles Dickens, Peter's career can be described as reflecting both the "best of men" and the "worst." Biblical passages may be found to describe his career as a disciple either way. Peter's confession of Christ as the Son of the living God represents Peter as the best of men, a faithful and trusting steward. Peter's denial of Jesus demonstrates how even the most promising career can falter under pressure.

Character Analysis

A sermon centering on character analysis is a study of the distinct personality traits of a biblical figure. The distinctives may be good or bad, but the character traits become the points of the sermon. The impulsiveness of Peter, the tenacity of Paul, the persistence of Jeremiah, the manic-depression of Elijah, the vices and virtues of David, the pettiness of Jonah, and the doubts of Thomas are all examples of how character analysis can provide the theme for a biographical sermon. The approaches to a biographical sermon are virtually unlimited. This brief summary cites only a few of the most popular approaches.

Narrative Sermons

Telling a story is a timeless way to communicate. A good story well told can totally involve listeners. As one observer comments: "When the story comes, in whatever form, there arises in us such a need to live in and to live ourselves into the story that we bend our imaginations, and, it would seem, our bodies as well, to the storyteller."[2] Narrative preaching, or the sermon-as-story, is not to be confused with simply telling *a* story. The purpose of narrated preaching is to tell the Story of stories. The gospel message is frequently referred to as "a story," and at least one favorite hymn speaks joyfully of telling "the old, old story of Jesus and his love." It is the gospel, *the* Story, to which narrative preaching really refers.

Much of the Bible is in narrative style, and these passages provide the most likely basis for narrative sermons. Any narrative, by definition, contains people and events. Careful attention to the CIT and Thesis will lead to an appropriate objective for a narrative sermon built from a text that tells a story about people and places and events. The sermon's objectives should be built on what is referred to as "the point" of the story. This is discovered by studying the background of the book from which the text is taken and from exegesis of the specific passages under consideration.

The structure of a sermon-as-story will be similar to that for any narrative in that it will include characters, events, and movement. Read any story in the Bible to see how the plot develops and the characters move within that framework. The parable of the waiting-father/prodigal-son/elder-brother is a good model. Notice in the text (Luke 15:11–32) the introduction of the characters: "A certain man had two sons." Notice the significant events: The younger son asked for his inheritance—departed—squandered his wealth—took a menial job—returned to his father repentantly—was welcomed back joyfully. A narrative sermon uses the same procedure, weaving together characters and events and moving them toward a resolution.

Delivering a narrative sermon should include strong qualities of vividness and even emotion—what is often called "being your natural self."

As one author advises, remember to:

> Think of yourself as a storyteller. . . . Think of yourself not as an orator, a rhetorician, or a pulpiteer, but as a storyteller.
>
> Don't simply *retell* an old story. Attempt to *recreate* it for your hearers. A real storyteller is not merely reporting something that happened or reciting what took place; the speaker is recreating the event with a view to enabling the hearers to relive the experience.[3]

Inductive Sermons

Should a sermon always be deductive? That is, should the preacher always *begin* with a biblical text (and its CIT, Objectives, and Thesis), which is then developed by explanation, application, and illustration? Not at all! It can be at least equally effective to use the reverse of this approach: the inductive sermon. This type of sermon begins with the congregation and moves toward the Scripture, as contrasted with the deductive method, which begins with Scripture and moves toward the life of the congregation. Either approach can be biblical. The deductive approach is more traditional, but inductive sermons can be just as valid.

Although the CIT-Objectives-Thesis furnish the "point" of the inductive sermon, they are not immediately presented. The inductive sermon, rather, begins with a life situation that is described and elaborated with a view to discovering some reconciliation or biblical principle related to the circumstances. That truth or principle is provided by the text at the end of the sermon. Harold Freeman explains:

> The inductive technique is like a nominating speech in which all of the content is stated in such a way that, by the time the speaker arrives at the point of announcing the nominee, the listener already knows who it is. In the inductive sermon, by the time the text is announced and explained, the thrust of the message has already become . . . clear. The sharing of the text and explanation of it serve to validate and authenticate the truth. [4]

Instead of reading the text at the beginning of the sermon, as in the deductive sermon, the text could be read at the end of the sermon. That way the reading of the text at the end of a sermon should be the climax in which the congregation finally perceives the point or main message. Such an approach can have significant positive impact on a congregation.

Application in an inductive sermon is usually stated at the beginning of the sermon (life situation) and then culminated with the reading of the text. The progression of the sermon begins with the life situation ("You are here"), gives a description of the situation ("This is what it feels like to be here"), and moves to a way to deal with the life situation, either by rejoicing in it or moving out of it (depending on the nature of the circumstances posited at the beginning of the sermon). Then the text is read and perhaps briefly explained. Finally the invitation is given, serving the purpose of re-emphasizing the application already presented.

Dialogue Sermons

Dialogue preaching is generally a planned (or scheduled) interaction between the preacher and members of the congregation. The format for planned dialogue preaching usually first involves the announcement of a subject for discussion and the reading of a biblical text by the preacher, followed by his or her comments or exposition of the text. The preacher then asks the congregation to respond by either asking questions about the subject and text and/or the preacher's comments or by making some additional observation about them. These remarks may agree or disagree with the preacher's comments. If the congregation is hesitant to volunteer, the preacher may call on specific individuals to respond.

The preacher must be especially careful with a congregational dialogue, not only to keep the "conversation" on target, but also to allow a variety of viewpoints to be aired. Some people will turn the dialogue into a monologue because of the length or frequency of their comments. The preacher should interrupt such speakers so as to maintain participation by a majority of the congregation. Others will try to deliver a diatribe on their favorite subject, no matter how unrelated that subject is to the sermon. The preacher should always be ready to remind such people that their comments are not pertinent. As for those people who are hesitant to speak, the preacher should be alert to opportunities to encourage them to express themselves.

Many congregations find dialogical preaching not particularly spiritually-oriented or worshipful. Or they may feel that the preacher should be sharing a word from God and not depending on the people to contribute their viewpoint. Most often, it is better to accede to the wishes of the congregation and not force a dialogue service on them. Although there are biblical and historical precedents for dialogical preaching, it may not be suitable for all congregations.

Technically-Aided Sermons

Using audio and visual aids is not new to twentieth-century preaching, although today's technology has expanded their potential. Objects from nature, handicrafts, chalk art, simply projected images, and even the Bible itself have been and still are used by preachers as visual aids. It has become increasingly easier to use a slide presentation to augment a sermon, and movies have even been used as entire sermons in some churches.

The audiovisually augmented sermon usually consists of a running monologue of explanation and application during which a specific object is displayed or demonstrated, a picture is drawn or shown, or slides are projected. Depending on the text and objectives of the sermon, a recording of music, sound effects, or the spoken word might also be played. It is important during this type of sermon to be sure that the monologue is in keeping with the objects or technology being used. Coordination between the spoken message and the audiovisual devices is essential so as to avoid trivializing the textual truths.

One of the chief problems with a technically augmented sermon is being sure that everyone in the audience is within viewing (and hearing) distance. Some sanctuaries and church auditoriums are built in a regimented rectangle. Congregational members seated at the rear of such a meeting place may have difficulty seeing the visual portion of the sermon. Other auditoriums are fan-shaped, which means that persons seated at either side may miss the impact of a visually illustrated example.

The use of audiovisual aids can be helpful to a congregation. Most of us can respond more strongly to what we see and hear directly than to what is merely described. Pragmatically, however, very few auditoriums are built so that such aids can be used effectively.

Variety in biblical preaching is highly recommended and should be the aim of all those called on to deliver God's message. The various sermon types included in this chapter are all biblically valid, and their effectiveness can be confirmed by various studies in communication. Of course, although any preacher should be flexible enough to try nontraditional methods, never use innovative preaching techniques merely to "shock" a congregation or try to show how "modern" you are. Not all fresh and unusual sermons will work with all congregations. Use new approaches to preaching only when you feel that they will enhance the effectiveness of the sermon.

Delivering the Message   8

As I have stipulated in a previous book, the guiding principle behind preaching—more specifically, sermon delivery—is to maximize the message and minimize the messenger. Content (*what* we preach) is always more important than delivery (*how* we preach).[1] We are commissioned to deliver an important message, and our delivery is *not* that message! When the focus of the sermon is the messenger instead of the message, a cultist following begins to be built around the personality of the preacher. The very existence of such admiration is a direct obstacle to receiving the message to be delivered. For a preacher to encourage a self-serving personality cult is as if the donkey who carried Jesus into Jerusalem thought the "hosannas" were for him. To call attention *to* the messenger is to force attention *away from* the message.

To "maximize the message and minimize the messenger," the preacher must refine the five major areas of sermon delivery: full vocal production, clear articulation, proper use of the vocal variables, body language, and oral interpretation.

Full Vocal Production

Full vocal production—often referred to as "diaphragmatic speaking"—is a process whereby a public speaker's voice can be used to its full potential and yet be protected from strain. Full vocal production uses tension in the strong abdominal muscles instead of in the delicate vocal bands within the larynx, thus protecting the voice from strain and possibly permanent harm. Although this type of vocalization can also make voices sound deeper and help preachers speak with tremendous volume, these side effects are incidental. The direct benefits of full vocal production are realizing the full potential of one's vocal equipment and protecting it from damage.

Full vocal production begins with breathing diaphragmatically. The diaphragm is a thin dome-shaped band of muscle in the upper abdominal area just beneath the lungs. The diaphragm is a "passive" muscle. As the lungs fill with air and expand (inhalation), the diaphragm is pushed down into a more flattened position. At the same time, the abdominal and rib muscles are pushed outward and become tense. This tension, or pressure, works against the diaphragm, which is then pushed upward against the lungs. The upward movement of the diaphragm causes increased air pressure in the lungs, thus bringing about exhalation, and the process of breathing is ready to repeat itself. By way of contrast, "shallow breathing" barely affects the diaphragm and will leave a preacher with too little air to achieve full vocal production. Check your own respiration: if your abdominal and rib muscles are not moving outward slightly during inhalation, your breathing is too shallow.

Full vocal production calls for controlled respiration, especially exhaling, on the part of the speaker. As air moves from the lungs past the vocal cords, several things happen simultaneously: the vocal bands vibrate to produce sounds; the sound is projected outward; and the sound is reinforced by reverberation in the chest, throat, nasal passages, and mouth. Each person is gifted with a distinct set of vocal cords. Vocal bands that vibrate at a low frequency produce a deeper sound than those vibrating more rapidly (producing a higher-pitched sound). If the air passes the vocal bands too rapidly, the sounds will be breathy. If air passes the vocal bands too slowly, vocal quality will lack smoothness. Essentially, the speaker must control his or her exhaling to produce a smooth, even, reinforced sound. This is the sound of full vocal production.

Because the vocal bands are delicate, they must be protected from strain. When the techniques of full vocal production are used, the preacher can expect to speak with a strong, clear voice and suffer no undesired aftereffects. When proper speech methods are not used, the preacher can expect frequent sore throats, laryngitis, a dull raspy voice, and, eventually, serious vocal problems that could terminate a preaching career and possibly require major surgery.[2] Full vocal production has one other important fringe benefit. The diaphragmatic breathing needed to achieve full vocal production provides a healthy level of oxygen to the body, which in turn helps relieve the tension or nervousness that is sometimes called stage fright.

Articulation

The sound produced by the vocalization process needs to be shaped into words if it is to be intelligible to others. This process is called articulation. The human tongue, lips, teeth, and palate are the bodily instruments used to shape vocal sounds into meaningful expression. There are forty-four speech sounds in the English language. To the degree that these sounds are articulated clearly, speech communication is enhanced.

It should be apparent that there are different perceptions as to what constitutes clear and acceptable articulation. Some misarticulated sounds result in what are called accents, usually thought of in regional terms. For example, in the northeastern United States articulated sounds are often formed at the front of the mouth and spoken so rapidly that some of the sounds are cut short. In the southern states, many articulated sounds are formed in the center of the mouth and spoken slowly, so that some of the sounds are prolonged. Both northeasterners and southerners pronounce the consonant r softly, while midwesterners give it a fuller sound. These generalizations are representative of the way in which accents are distinguished within the United States.

There are four basic types of misarticulation:

1. Omission of sounds. This is common with words that end in "ing," as in "preachin'" instead of preaching.

2. Substitution of sounds. For example, "jist" instead of "just," "git" for "get," "fer" instead of "for," and "becuz" instead of "because."

3. Distortion of sounds. Notice the distortion of "I" into "Ah," or "oil" into "erl."

4. Addition of sounds. Common examples here include "warsh" for "wash" or "Ath-uh-lete" for "athlete."

Most misarticulations are due to lazy speech habits. To correct these habits, the first step is to consult a speech book which describes each of the forty-four speech sounds. These descriptions may then be applied to words containing the individual sounds. The preacher will want to correct misarticulations that may be hindering his or her sermon delivery.

Vocal Variables

The four vocal variables are pitch, volume, rate, and pauses. Used in variety in a way that supports a sermon's content, vocal variables can aid in communicating the total message. Although these variables work in tandem with one another and there is almost no limit to the variety of ways that they can be used, each will be discussed separately.

It is extremely important to note that the vocal variables are largely responsible for communicating the emotional impact of a sermon. Every form of oral communication, especially a sermon, carries both an intellectual message and an emotional message. The intellectual message is the content which essentially is delivered by the words and syntax used. The emotional message communicates how the preacher feels about the content and thus how his listeners should feel about what is said. Actually, the intellectual message itself can have emotional impact, as in "God is like a father to us." In this example, even when the emotional message of the preacher conveys warmth and appreciation, the word *father* may elicit an opposite feeling in some listeners. One unfortunate member of the congregation may reflect: "God is like a father? My father abuses me. Who needs a god like that?" In such a case, the intellectual message carries emotional baggage that is beyond the immediate control of the preacher.

A public speaker must try to anticipate what sort of emotions the intellectual message may arouse in the audience. This is especially important in preaching. Once the intellectual message is prepared, the preacher must be careful to communicate an emotional message that correlates with the intellectual content. This is done by effective use of the vocal variables described below.

Pitch

The first variable, pitch, refers to the tonal qualities of vocal sounds and there are five factors involved: optimum level, range, interval, intonation, and inflection.

Optimum pitch level is simply the appropriate average pitch level for an individual's vocal apparatus. This can be easily identified by singing down the musical scale to the lowest note that can be comfortably vocalized. From that lowest note, go back up five notes. This is close to the pitch that you should recognize as your optimum level, the quality at which it is most natural and comfortable for you to speak most of the time.

Pitch range refers to a speaker's breadth of pitch level above and below his or her optimum pitch. A wide pitch range can provide the preacher with considerable vocal agility in support of a sermon's content.

Pitch interval involves the distance between two consecutive pitch levels used in speaking two words or within one word. Varying the pitch levels keeps sermon delivery from being a dull monotone.

Pitch intonation refers to the pitch range used within a phrase or sentence. Effectively delivering content calls for variety in intonation. However, many preachers fall into a habitual intonation pattern, which may become dull or annoying to the audience. When patterning occurs, the preacher needs to build a stronger relationship between intonation and the message being communicated.

Pitch inflection refers to the movement from one pitch level within a word or even within a syllable. Varieties in inflection are as useful in communicating the emotional message found in a sermon as are the other pitch variables.

Volume

The volume variable, or loudness, refers to the amount of force used in delivering the message. Volume must be adjusted so as to support content and simultaneously be suitable for the size and acoustical qualities of the worship area. The preacher should use higher or lower volume as the sermon's content dictates. For instance, when making an emphatic theological assertion, a forceful delivery would be appropriate. The preacher should never cause people to strain to listen, but neither should a congregation be blasted into shell shock by an overly loud interjection or thundering comment.

Rate

The rate—or speed—at which a person speaks is usually measured in words per minute. The average speaking rate is between 125 and 150 words per minute. A fairly rapid rate is usually used for familiar, elementary, or nonessential material. Slower speech is necessary for unfamiliar, complex, or emphatic material. Varying the speaking rate either above or below the average range allows a preacher to achieve the emotional effect appropriate to the content of the message.

Pauses

Judiciously placed pauses work together with rate to produce "phrasing." Pauses are separations between words, phrases, sentences, or paragraphs. When brief, pauses last about one second and serve to allow listeners time to keep track of the steady stream of words. Intermediate pauses (one to three seconds) are used primarily to make a transition from one thought to another or to allow a little more time for facts or ideas to be absorbed. Long pauses (three to five seconds) usually indicate a change in thought, but they are also used effectively to gain attention. Occasionally, pauses are vocalized. That is unfortunate because vocalization actually destroys the pause's impact. Since preachers communicate uncertainty when they use "uh," "er," or "you know," the only really effective pauses are silent and intentional ones.

Someone will probably someday invent a machine that will help preachers measure the effectiveness of the vocal variables used during their sermon delivery. Ideally, this machine would record every word of the sermon on a horizontal sheet of paper. Beneath each word of the sermon, four lines in different colors would graphically record the use of pitch, volume, rate, and pauses. Such a graph would enable the preacher to see how he or she used each of the vocal variables in relation to every word of the sermon. The preacher could then evaluate how well the delivery supported the content of the sermon. If the graph registered a high level of rate, pitch, and volume in one section, the preacher could evaluate whether the words at that point actually required such levels. If the words of the sermon were urgent and vital, perhaps a high level of rate, pitch, and volume was appropriate. If the words were used only to make a transition or were secondary to the main thrust of the sermon, high readings for those vocal variables were probably not appropriate. Effective use of these speech tech-

niques can more strongly communicate both the intellectual
and the emotional message of any sermon.

Body Language

Nonverbal communication, or body language, is important
in conveying a message, but much more subtle than the vocal
variables involved in the delivery process. Body language primarily includes facial expressions, gestures, posture, and eye
contact. Although these visible signals must also support content and usually work in concert with vocal variables, it is
possible for body language to communicate in silence. A smile,
a frown, a shrug of the shoulders, a slump in posture—all
communicate without a word being spoken. Whether or not
body language is correlated with a spoken message, it is always communicating. The preacher must strive to express
body language that always supports—and never contradicts—
sermon content.

Facial Expressions

If a person's eyes were truly windows to the soul, nothing
further would need to be said about the importance of facial
expressions in preaching. The truth is, facial expressions can
communicate an amazing range of emotions. During the delivery of a sermon preachers can see their own gestures and
posture, but not their facial expressions. It is difficult for any
preacher to know if a smile or frown, for instance, is as obvious as it feels. When viewing a videotape of themselves, many
preachers are surprised to note that their faces are virtually
expressionless and do not reflect their feelings. Some preachers, though gifted in their ability to be open and free in conveying their emotions verbally, need to practice in front of a
mirror until their facial expressions—smiles, frowns, gri-
maces—are truly reflective of what they feel.

Gestures

Gestures can include any part of the body but generally indicate hands-and-arms activity. Since gestures are impulsive movements that reflect the speaker's feelings, they are a valuable tool in supporting the content of a sermon. There are a few basic gestures that are almost universally understood. For example, "palms up" communicates acceptance or a positive response; "palms down" shows rejection or calls for a negative response. Broad insweeping gestures communicate inclusiveness and camaraderie. A clenched fist or a pointed finger can be used for emphasis or decisiveness. Whether spontaneous or deliberate, effective gestures support content and are timed to correspond with vocal variables and the other aspects of body language. Gestures are distracting when they do not relate to content, when there are so many that they become a blur of motion, or when they are repetitious or rhythmic and thus seem rehearsed and forced.

Posture

Good posture should be comfortable to the speaker but not distracting to the audience. Body stance, therefore, should be neither rigid nor slouchy. The position of the feet is important to good posture. Although individual speakers will need to determine their own best position, it is recommended that one foot be slightly forward of the other (use whichever foot seems most comfortable). When weight is placed on the forward foot, the preacher's body is inclined slightly toward the congregation and communicates a sense of urgency. When weight is placed on the back foot, one's body leans slightly away from the congregation. This sends a message of rejection. (To summarize: body forward + palms up + perhaps a smile = a sense of acceptance. And body leaning back + palms down + perhaps a frown = a sense of rejection.)

Placing one foot forward of the other also has the advantage of limiting body sway. A nervous preacher, with feet side by side, will sometimes shift weight rapidly from one foot to the other. This causes a swaying motion that is extremely distracting to a congregation. Of course, the position of the feet or any other aspect of posture can be changed during the sermon to make it more appropriate to the content and emotional message of the sermon.

Eye Contact

Since eye contact is extremely important to the congregation, look directly toward the eyes of your listeners. Do not dwell on any one person or a particular section, but avoid sweeping across the congregation too rapidly. Establish eye contact before the first words of the sermon are spoken, then plan to maintain this contact for 80 to 90 percent of the sermon's duration.

One of the main problems for preachers is breaking eye contact to look at notes at the end of a key assertion. This disconnection during a major point in the sermon is usually accompanied by a lapse in vocal expression and body language. Always complete the important statement vocally, maintain eye contact during a medium-length pause, then continue the pause as you glance at notes, reestablish eye contact, and begin to speak again. This is not as mechanical as it sounds. The congregation will hardly notice the process because they will be absorbing the key assertion.

Body language is a coordinated activity that serves visually to support the vocally transmitted content of the sermon. Body language can be planned and practiced, but it should always appear to be spontaneous. Whenever body language calls attention to itself by lack of spontaneity, it has defeated its purpose. Whenever body language subtly reinforces the content of the sermon, it is working well.

Oral Interpretation

The principles of oral interpretation—the art of reading literature aloud—apply perfectly to sermon delivery. Oral interpretation brings all the elements of delivery together. As we have seen, these include full vocal production, clear articulation, proper use of the vocal variables, and effective application of body language. For the preacher, oral interpretation is specifically needed in *reading* Scripture, but the principles apply also to a sermon or, in fact, *publicly speaking* any message.

Reading Scripture

During your planning time, first determine the nature of the Scripture passage to be read and then set the general pace and mood accordingly. Narrative passages, for example, may be read a little more rapidly than poetic literature. Narratives have setting, plot, and characters and are therefore usually easier for a congregation to follow.

As you prepare, read the passage aloud several times and focus on the main words of the text. A simple exercise to accomplish this is alternately emphasizing one word while de-emphasizing the others. Vocal emphasis can be made by pausing before the word, setting a higher pitch inflection, and/or using higher volume. For instance, in the Luke 15 passage beginning "Jesus continued, 'There was a man who had two sons . . .' " the name *Jesus* could be emphasized and all other words downplayed. Try this aloud and see how it sounds, then try emphasizing the word *continued* instead. Repeat this exercise for each word in the sentence. You may decide that none of the words needs emphasis. Jesus' identity has already been established, and the word *continued* ("said" in some versions) simply points to the quote to come and does not call for emphasis (except as it connects this parable to the previous one). The quote itself simply leads in to a more important lesson. Try saying the passage with a slight emphasis on the word *two*. In the next verse put a slight emphasis on the word *younger*. This type of exercise will help you, the reader, perceive the meaning of the passage and be better equipped to orally convey that meaning to a congregation.

Remember that the purpose of oral interpretation is to *suggest* meaning, not circumscribe listener response. Let the congregation develop mental images. It is not advisable for the preacher to display or dramatize the meaning, although it is permissible to use vocal expressions and body language to imply the meaning of the Scripture being read.

Preaching the Sermon

The same principles used for reading Scripture can be broadly adapted to preaching. Here, the "literature" is a sermon. The main words of the sermon are emphasized just as they are in reading Scripture. The preacher in this way can suggest the meaning of the sermon to the congregation.

Guidelines for Mass Media

All the previously mentioned principles of sermon preparation and delivery are applicable to preaching on radio and television. Still, there are a couple of important principles the preacher should know about radio and television.

First, the clock is a ruthless and unbending dictator to broadcasters. Respect the station's need to abide by strict time limits. It is important that the program end exactly at the scheduled time—not "a little" before or after.

Second, the broadcaster is legally responsible for everything that is said (or shown) through the local station or channel. Be careful not to embarrass the station executives, cause complications, or bring about legal difficulties for them. The station management can brief the preacher on current Federal Communications Commission laws. The preaching of the gospel in and of itself will rarely cause the broadcaster any problems. But if a preacher expresses a partisan view on certain controversial side issues, the local station may be obliged to allot "equal time" to the other side.

The delivery of the sermon is as important as the vehicle that delivers a precious cargo. The vehicle should do its job so smoothly that no one notices the vehicle and concentrates on the cargo. For the preacher the message is the cargo, and sermon delivery is the vehicle. Sermon delivery should be done so efficiently that congregations are more involved with the message than they are with delivery of the message.

Improving the Dynamics

9

In addition to sermon preparation and delivery, a preacher has responsibilities in related areas and should be equipped to provide leadership as required. These areas include evaluating previous sermons, maintaining pulpit decorum, meeting with pastoral search committees, and responding to a new preaching opportunity. In addition, some preachers serve as military chaplains or must preach through an interpreter. Most conduct funeral sermons. It seems appropriate in this final chapter to add some ideas about these matters and also some suggestions regarding establishing a filing system for sermons, how to re-preach a sermon, how to use another's ideas in a sermon, and finally, what to do when it seems there is no fresh word from the Lord.

Last Sunday's Sermon

Most preachers evaluate the effectiveness of a sermon by counting the number of persons who directly express a positive response. Although there should be no minimizing the importance of this feedback, this is a very limited way to measure the impact of a sermon.

Preachers would be wise also to do some self-evaluation that involves simple analysis of the most recent sermon(s). It is helpful to make a videotape (or oral recording) of the sermon and then transcribe portions of the sermon from the tape. (Transcribing means to write down every word and sound as it is uttered on the tape.) The portions of the sermon selected for transcription should be those where the preacher felt some improvement was needed. Transcribing causes the preacher to relive specific moments by seeing which words were used and how they were delivered. (Personally, transcribing a portion of my sermons and analyzing the transcription as described is the single most expeditious way of improving the quality of my preaching that I have ever done.) Such analysis helps the preacher evaluate context and delivery at the same time. This type of evaluation has an immediate and beneficial impact on anyone who has worked through it. The result, in most cases, is preaching that is stronger and clearer than before. Any preacher would be proud to have the epitaph, "This messenger of God preached a strong, clear message." Transcribing just two paragraphs per sermon virtually guarantees noticeable improvement in the content and delivery of future preaching.

One preacher used this process and shared it as an example of the way transcribing a portion of a sermon can be immediately beneficial. The numbers within the transcription were made by the preacher as he listened to the tape. The numbers are decoded beneath the transcription.

As we have seen then Paul wrote in strong contrast when he wrote, ". . . but the gift of God is eternal life through Jesus Christ our Lord"[1] which we are not to take for granted as some people are prone to take for granted even the things of God who . . . uh[2] . . . would never be taken for granted . . . just as . . . uh . . .[3] we should not take our families for granted including our parents and God, of course, is like a father to us, but I must return to the subject at hand.[4]

The word "but" is a word of strong contrast. The contrast between the first part of this verse and the second part of this verse is a kind of night and day contrast—it is literally a death/life contrast.[5]

1. *This is where a new thought suddenly came to mind and I ran with it. I should have stayed with the main theme of the sermon.*

2. *Now I realize that I am into "taking things for granted" and that has nothing to do with my sermon. I remember thinking as I was preaching, "How did I get here, and how do I get out of here."*

3. *My delivery is very poor here—choppy, monotone, loss of eye contact. I was restructuring the sermon while I was talking.*

4. *An eighty-seven word sentence! How can I expect my people to be moved when even on replay I don't understand what I just heard myself say!*

5. *I am a little sharper here. I can hear the confidence returning. I think I tend to be a little didactic, though.*

This preacher later testified that his preaching becomes much smoother and sharper after he started evaluating his sermons by transcribing portions of those he had most recently preached. Significantly, he also shared that now his congregation frequently discussed his sermons intelligently and approvingly. Finally, he stated proudly, he had never again come even close to an eighty-seven-word sentence!

Pulpit Decorum

Most preachers learn pulpit decorum from mentors or others they have selected as role models. A good role model in preaching should provide a worthy example of how to dress appropriately, how to maintain dignity without seeming to be stodgy, how best to participate in worship before and after the sermon, and how to handle distractions during the sermon.

Appropriate Dress for the Pulpit

The basic rule here is to avoid clothing that by calling attention to itself places emphasis on the messenger rather than the message. This guideline rules out extremely bright colors, some nefarious color combinations, and certain flashy types or styles of clothing. For example, motivational research indicates that a male preacher (if not wearing a clerical collar) whose suit color is dark blue (especially navy), black, or gray best communicates a sense of authority (*not* "authoritarianism"). In that case, a long-sleeved shirt, usually in white, would also convey that feeling. The reasons for these conclusions are too numerous to mention, but congregations seem to expect their preachers to be dressed conservatively, especially when in the pulpit, although this may vary regionally and according to the type of community. When there is a special reason for not wearing a suit—or a simple tailored dress, if the preacher is a woman—congregations will understand and accept less formal clothing. Nevertheless, its style should basically reflect what is commonly worn within the congregation. For example, although a three-piece suit would be the norm for men in some areas, a western-style pants and jacket would be more appropriate in others.

Some independent-thinking preachers insist that people should not "judge the book by its cover," a rationalization often used to be avant-garde or to resist established trends. The fact of the matter is—fairly or not—that some judgment is made by congregations on how the preacher is dressed.

Grooming is part of the total picture, so take time to look in a mirror before making a public appearance. If a man, your tie should be straight, hair combed, shoes polished, and, by all means, make the X-Y-Z (Examine Your Zipper) test! A woman in the pulpit should avoid complicated hair styles and heavy makeup and leave bright or jangling jewelry at home. Rather than complicate the preaching situation with details that should be incidental to the sermon, the preacher's appearance should never be such as to allow the congregation to lose sight of the message.

Closely related to the matter of appropriate dress is personal hygiene. For example, congregations understand perspiration, but they may not fathom why perspiration is allowed to become offensive and rarely tolerate preachers who go unbathed. Congregations also presume that all adults will wash their hands after a visit to the toilet and that therefore a warm handshake will carry nothing more than a sense of Christian fellowship. It is simply amazing that elementary instruction is often needed by some preachers in the area of personal hygiene! For most people, such lessons were learned and practiced since kindergarten. Since those of us who practice good hygiene are acutely aware of those who do not, you will no doubt understand why this simple reminder is included here.

Participation in Worship

Proper pulpit behavior calls for the preacher to be a full participant in the worship service. When the congregation sings, the preacher should be joining in. When there is special music, the preacher should be inspired by it (or at least appear to be). When the congregation is called to prayer by another pastoral or lay official, the preacher should be praying with them. In this way, when the preacher steps up to share the sermon, he or she is in step and in spirit with the total worship experience. The preacher, of course, will often lead the time of prayer and may be a soloist or participate in some way in the special music. However, when not directly involved in a specific activity, the preacher should be a full participant by listening and worshiping. It is extremely distracting to see the preacher making or reviewing sermon notes or otherwise involved in extraneous matters during worship. Such actions may make the congregation feel the preacher is not totally prepared to preach.

While seated on the platform, a preacher is usually well advised to sit straight, with both feet on the floor. The eye level of the congregation is almost always such that it is awkward for the preacher to sit cross-legged while facing them from a raised position. Try not to be rigid in appearance on the platform, but instead maintain a relaxed dignity that does not call attention to itself—or to you.

Handling Distractions

Occasionally distractions occur during a sermon. Stories abound about public-address systems that temporarily pick up signals from a passing C.B. or local ham radio operator. Then there are the birds, animals, and insects that inadvertently enter the worship area. Perhaps a modern Eutychus (see Acts 20:9–12) dozes off in the congregation or, worse, in the choir. Sometimes a crying or restless child or a sudden medical emergency claims the congregation's attention.

There is no particularly recommended way to handle a distraction so as to guarantee a minimum of interruption to the sermon. Whenever possible, ignore the distraction. Since a minor diversion may be obvious only to some of the congregation, acknowledging it would make everyone aware of it.

When the distraction cannot be ignored, deal with it with humor if that is appropriate. This can quickly minimize the adverse effect and allow attention to be focused on the sermon again. When humor is not fitting, take a leadership stance and call for removing the distraction or, if necessary, cancel the remainder of the sermon. In a medical emergency, for instance, the preacher may have to instruct some people to assist in securing first aid and ask others to be in prayer for the afflicted person. Depending on the severity of the emergency (and assuming that medical treatment is obtained), it may be better to continue in prayer until the close of the service rather than trying to finish the interrupted sermon.

Avoid scolding people from the pulpit! The person who fell asleep, the parents of a restless child, or a whispering and giggling group of teenagers may or may not need to be reprimanded. However, a public reprimand will have diminishing returns for the preacher. The person or persons involved will be humiliated and probably will never be able to return to worship without remembering that humiliation. Whenever possible, do the scolding afterward—and privately rather than publicly.

Pastoral Search Committees

The pastoral search committee has an awesome responsibility. A preacher targeted for evaluation as a pastoral candidate can be helpful—or detrimental—to the search committee's efforts to fulfill its responsibility. There are three basic ways you can be helpful if you find yourself in that situation:

1. *Preach to the congregation for whom the sermon was prepared.* The search committee needs to see a preacher in relation to a congregation. Preaching just to a committee, in hopes of favorably impressing them, usually has the opposite result. In addition, this kind of preaching unforgivably belittles the message and the objectives of the search. The pastoral search committee can much more accurately determine God's will by observing your interaction with a congregation in a natural setting.

2. *Be a gracious host.* Most members of a search committee will feel a sense of trepidation or apology for imposing themselves on a preacher's life. You make them feel more comfortable by arranging a time and place to visit with them if that is their desire. You can usually help the committee most by answering their questions in a direct manner, although even as a candidate you may have to suggest appropriate questions to be asked. Be sure that the committee has clear direction to overnight accommodations (if necessary), to restaurants and to the highways they will use in returning to their home base.

3. *Be honest with the committee.* Tell the visitors whether or not you are sure about your interest in their church. Tell the committee if you are presently dealing with any other search groups. If called, respond to the committee as soon as possible so as not to leave them in limbo about your decision. Never allow yourself to degenerate to the point where you use the visit or interest of a pastoral search committee as leverage to manipulate your present congregation in any way. Conversely, never use the love and respect of your congregation to win promises from the visiting committee. These self-serving

actions should be beneath any preacher's dignity and required level of servanthood.

New Opportunities

The first sermons preached in a new preaching opportunity will be foundational to a continuing ministry in that situation. To establish a strong foundation, the preacher should be thoroughly informed about the nature and history of the church, mission, parish, chaplaincy, or whatever the setting of the new opportunity may be. Such information may be found in a recent "history," one of which is usually written periodically by most ecclesiastical groups.[1] Reading such a localized history may point to specific areas of need within the congregation, or may explain some "traditions" that a new preacher would do well to respect. When a historical account is not available, a perusal of the minutes of several business meetings can serve the same purpose. In addition, conversations with various members of the congregation will usually provide an oral history that will help a preacher "feel the pulse" of the parishioners.

The initial sermons in any new setting should probably be limited to basic doctrinal studies. Even though many members of the audience are familiar with the broad tenets of the faith, the first sermons will establish a solid foundation for the ministry if they are directed to the nature of the Bible, God, Jesus, the Holy Spirit, the church universal, salvation, eschatology, and so on. These introductory sermons are at best a means of uniting the congregation and preacher in preparation for years of fruitful ministry. At the very least they are a reminder and affirmation of the matters of belief that underscore the fellowship of Christian believers.

The Military Chaplain

Preaching in a military chapel is a unique challenge. Consider the ingredients. As in any secularly defined community, a large segment of the "parish" of a military chaplain is not worship-oriented. Those who are interested in worship represent an extreme diversity of socioeconomic, ethnic, and religious backgrounds. ("Protestant," for instance, includes everyone who is not Roman Catholic or Jewish.) To complicate the task further, the nucleus of the congregation affiliated with the chapel has been on base for a relatively short time and will likely soon be transferred elsewhere. Therefore, on every preaching occasion, the military chaplain faces diversity without continuity. Nevertheless, there are some constants in preaching that will help the chaplain:

1. *Follow the guidelines for biblical preaching.* The basic steps for sermon preparation as outlined in this book are as valid for the military chaplain as for any other preacher. Every congregation needs a word from the Lord. A clear biblical sermon with contemporary application will always be appropriate and appreciated. In fact, preaching strong Scripture-oriented sermons can rapidly bring people of diverse backgrounds together and motivate them toward a common goal.

2. *Maintain a warm personal stance in the pulpit.* Help the congregation realize that you are preaching to them individually and that you see each person as a unique person in Christ. This approach will help overcome the ethereal sense of anonymity that is found in many military relationships. If your listeners feel that your sermon is just another exercise in impersonal mass media, their response will be severely limited. Also, a chaplain must guard against preaching just to impress one individual or in a way that is perceived as seeking to obtain a promotion. Remember, a sermon is meant to bring together the Word of God and the needs of the people. The preacher cannot disregard either the Word or the people. One of the fastest-growing movements in military worship services is known as the Gospel Service. One of the reasons for the rapid growth of this type of service is the feeling of being able to relate personally rather than just professionally.

3. *Be open to variety in sermon format.* This "variety," again, should not simply be for the sake of novelty. Rather,

the diverse nature of the congregation calls for seeking as many appealing approaches to the sermon as the preacher can muster. Variety in sermon organization and technique broadens the appeal of the message, eradicates predictability in the chapel service, and thereby increases the sense of anticipation the congregation brings to the chapel week by week.

A preacher who feels led to the military chaplaincy must be ever open to new ideas rather than steeped in a particular liturgical tradition. Fortunately, the gospel, though an unchanging story, thrives on being presented in any way that can make vital contact with people. The military chaplain has the challenge of preaching this timeless message in both creative and traditional ways.

Preaching Through an Interpreter

Preaching with the help of a translator to a congregation that does not understand the English language is a special challenge. The following guidelines are essential:

1. *Prepare a sermon that is briefer than usual.* Obviously, any sermon will take twice as long to deliver if it is being spoken twice. The preacher, therefore, should prepare a sermon that is about one-half the average length of sermons preached only in English.

2. *Be sensitive to cultural differences.* Do not presume, for instance, that North American humor will be understood and appreciated in other cultures. Do some research, and consult the interpreter for guidance on cultural differences.

3. *Be direct.* Every message will suffer a little in translation. It is much easier to convey a simple, straightforward message than it is an abstract, complicated one.

Funeral Preaching

A funeral address is part eulogy and part sermon. This preaching may be delivered in two separate segments but is often blended into one message of consolation. There are some basic guidelines for preparing a funeral message:

1. *Phrase the message in terms of mercy and grace.* Address the remarks to the living, not to the dead! Present will be some mourners who regularly attend worship services and others who rarely attend, but a message about God's grace will always be appropriate. John 14 is the most popular text for the message of grace.

2. *Share a brief eulogy.* In the freshness of their grief, most mourners need to hear a few public words about the deceased. It is comforting to hear someone else's perception of the deceased and to know that his or her memory is being honored. Note that the virtues of the loved one can be mentioned without being laudatory or maudlin.

3. *Do not dwell on pitiful circumstances.* The purpose of the funeral message is consolation, not to evoke painful emotions.

4. *Plan to speak for only six to eight minutes.* The consolation delivered in the funeral message will have either an immediate impact or none at all. A prolonged funeral message only drains the mourners emotionally.

5. *Be in contact with the grieving family both before and after the funeral service.* Contact before the service will assist the preacher in preparing the funeral message. The contact afterward will add a personal touch that will enhance consolation for the family.

6. *If the deceased was a Christian, magnify that fact in the hope that others will follow that course.* This type of funeral is a victory service. There is, to be sure, sorrow at the loss, but this sorrow is greatly tempered by the living hope of eternal blessings.

7. *If the deceased was not a Christian, it is better not to say anything about his or her ultimate future.* Some preachers practice a sympathetic universalism by making predictions that God's love prevails even where it is rejected. Such a practice is a mockery that costs the preacher much credibility. Other preachers dwell on the fact that the deceased was

not a Christian, thus adding to the sorrow of the family by specifying the uncertain future of the departed loved one. Much reserve ought to be exercised in this type of funeral service.

Filing Sermons

Sermons ought to be preserved. Whether on computer disc, electronic tape, paper, or all three, every sermon should be saved for future reference. The sermon represents an investment in exegetical work, in insights into scripture as it relates to the congregation, and in illustrative material. In short, a sermon is simply too valuable to be discarded, especially since it may be preached again someday, albeit with some updating and improvement.

A particular sermon will also be a way of measuring one's homiletical growth. Many preachers read their early sermons with some embarrassment and a degree of sympathy for the congregations who heard them. At the same time, the preacher may look at previous sermons and realize that maturity, experience, and ever-expanding knowledge are gradually accumulating to make him or her a more effective bearer of God's message.

A few preachers can trust their memories. Herschel H. Hobbs, for example, testifies that he never repeats an illustration to the same congregation because something in his memory facilitates cataloging and using illustrative material. Systems for filing sermons vary with the preacher. Some use computers for elaborately detailed systems of indexing and cross-referencing by both biblical texts and sermon subjects. Other preachers simply file their sermons mechanically, either by text or by topic.

Filing with a computerized system of indexing is not so much complicated as it is time-consuming. Care must be taken that the topical listings do not overlap. Here is where comprehensive cross-referencing can help. Otherwise a preacher may, for example, seek vainly for a past sermon on the subject of

"Trust," only to find later that the sermon he wanted had been filed under "Faith." Or a missing sermon on "Salvation" may later be found under "Atonement." When care (and perhaps a thesaurus) is used, cross-references can be extremely useful as a locating tool.

Filing by biblical text is simple but limited in application. This system includes every book of the Bible, with sermons filed according to passage reference. A sermon with Romans 6:23 as a text is filed under Romans, as also is a sermon on Romans 12:1–2. If references to a given biblical text are all that a preacher would ever require, this filing system might be adequate. The limitation is that various sermon subjects are grouped under the same listing. For example, under the computer entry of "Romans," the screen might simply indicate the texts within Romans for which the preacher has prepared sermons:

Romans

Romans 3:23
Romans 6:23
Romans 8:1–5
Romans 8:28
Romans 12:1–2

This listing of texts would probably include sermons preached evangelistically, doctrinally, supportively, and consecratively. The text references alone say nothing about the content of the sermon or its objectives.

An indexing system that uses books of the Bible as filing categories could be easily expanded by adding just a little more information:

Romans

Romans 3:23 An evangelistic sermon emphasizing the depravity of humanity

Romans 6:23 An evangelistic sermon contrasting the hopeless life of a non-Christian and the hope-filled life of a Christian

Romans 8:1–5 A doctrinal sermon on the qualities of a Spirit-filled Christian

Romans 8:28 A supportive sermon to help when bad things happen to good people

Romans 12:1–2 A challenge to Christians to live the Christian life to the full

Every preacher is capable of designing a filing system to fill his or her own requirements. These suggestions are shared to get you started in developing an individualized method for preserving sermons.

Preaching Sermons Again

Should a sermon ever be preached more than once? Certainly! The question is raised only because of the potential for abuse. A sermon should not be repeated if the preacher is simply trying to avoid the labor of preparation. When considering whether to preach a sermon on a second occasion, the preacher is obligated to pray diligently for divine guidance. Is *this* sermon what *this* congregation needs at *this* time? If God's answer to that prayer is affirmative, the preacher should then spend time and consideration on the following ideas:

1. *Review the notes (or manuscript) for the original sermon and any evaluation made after the sermon was first preached.* This review will help you recognize how much of the sermon's explanation (or biblical exposition) needs to be improved and how much its general clarity needs sharpening.

2. *Review the application of the sermon.* How may the application be made more pertinent and contemporary to this congregation? Some revisions may help improve the force and appeal of the sermon.

3. *Review the illustrative material.* Some illustrations are

timeless; others are dated. For instance, replace an illustration that excitedly reported the successful launching of Sputnik I with a more recent achievement in space.

4. *Aim for freshness of expression.* Otherwise, preaching the sermon again may merely be an exercise in memorization. Any sermon must be fresh and exciting to the preacher before it can have that same effect on the congregation. Every time a sermon is preached again, its content should mature and objectives crystallize so that each re-preaching is more exciting than the last.

5. *Do not apologize for preaching the sermon again.* If you have been led to repeat a sermon, and have actually reworked it for a specific congregation or occasion, no apologies are necessary.

Using Other's Thoughts[2]

Even the most effective preachers are inspired by the sermons of others and have been "led" to borrow ideas or illustrative material from them. This process has varied from preacher to preacher. At one extreme are preachers who hear a sermon that merely triggers a sermon topic in their own minds. These preachers then personally work this inspiration through in their preparation procedures. At the other extreme are the preachers who actually plagiarize-point-by-point, illustration-by-illustration, sometimes word-for-word the messages of other preachers. It is no wonder that for several decades such preachers have bragged that when better sermons are preached, *they* will preach them, too! Although most of us stop short of deliberately pilfering, there are some guidelines for using the sermons of other preachers with integrity.

1. *Be "inspired," but do not copy.* The impact made by someone else's sermon may lead a preacher to prepare a sermon on the same subject, with the same text, and possibly with some of the same insights and objectives. However, these elements should be expressed in his or her own words. To do this, the preacher will be forced to process the inspiring ma-

terial through his or her own unique experiences. The result will be the appropriation of another person's sermon by *adapting* it to one's own life. With that dynamic in operation, a sermon becomes a part of the preacher.

2. *Give credit when credit is due.* There may be occasions when the insights of a sermon are so fresh and creative that the only good way to use the ideas is to repeat them almost verbatim. Whenever your dependence on another's work is so obvious, a brief acknowledgment should be made, sometimes quite specifically: "A Billy Graham sermon on the Second Coming spoke to me in a special way. I will be using some of his thoughts in today's message." Or the acknowledgment may call for more generality: "I recently was moved by reading an English Baptist preacher's sermon on this text and will be borrowing some of his thoughts for today's message." If someone should ask, "*Which* English Baptist preacher?" you should, of course, be prepared to name him. Unless your congregation would recognize the name if you offered it, the less specific acknowledgment would usually be preferable.

3. *Be especially conscious of using illustrative material with integrity.* The power of some sermons may be almost entirely built on the personal and unique experience of the original author. Do not use that illustration without strong acknowledgment as to its source. Never imply that *you* are the person who lived through that experience firsthand. If you do, you will not need to wonder whether you have crossed the acceptable limits of fair play—you have!

Remember, plagiarism consists of taking someone else's work (or any part thereof) and representing it as your own. Plagiarism is a dishonest practice that reflects a loss of integrity and eventually leads to a loss of credibility. The Christian pulpit cannot tolerate either deficiency.

When You Have "No Word from the Lord"

Every preacher has experienced spiritual drought for varying reasons, sometimes because of overwork. Preachers are prone to see their jobs as an avocation, but—as pleasant as it is to love your work—the constant pressure of preaching and pastoral duties will occasionally bring on a time of non-productivity. Whatever the reason for such a dry spell, con-gregations still arrive on Sundays as regularly as sunrise, with the expectation of hearing a word from the Lord through you—his messenger.

So what do you do when you do not feel a message from the Lord? Some preachers show a movie, and a well-produced, appropriately chosen film can be inspirational to a congre-gation. Others would rather dismiss the worship service at the point a sermon would ordinarily be scheduled. The con-gregation enjoys music and prayer together and then, instead of a sermon, receives the pastor's announcement, "I do not have a word from the Lord for you today, so we will now sing our final hymn." Surely, there is a better solution to the dilemma!

When you truly feel that you do not have a fresh word from the Lord, return to the last word you had from him and preach that.[3] *Your* spiritual drought does not mean that God has run out of messages for your congregation. The dearth of new insights from God often means that the last word you received from him needs to be preached some more. This observation should be comforting to preachers who have agonized for hours and even days looking for the divine guidance that will spark their spirits and kindle a sermon into flame. Any preacher who is in spiritual limbo on Friday and Saturday wants to feel spiritually definite for Sunday. Do not dismiss the congrega-tion with a blunt announcement that "God does not have a word for us today. Or if he does I do not know what it is." God always has a word for his people.

One other comment about spiritual drought: it is forever amazing how God can bless a service even when the preacher feels that he or she fumbled, stuttered, felt arid and empty. I know of one such pastor who was tempted to apologize to the congregation for what he thought came across as ineptitude. Then he realized that the people were deeply moved. After the sermon, many came by to say that it was the most powerful sermon they had ever heard. Yet he had felt he was "doing a miserable job." Such occasions are beautiful reminders to us that it is often when we are at the end of ourselves that God's love is expressed most clearly and powerfully. Before every sermon, we preachers can join the apostle John in the sentiment, "Even so, come, Lord Jesus!"

Appendix A

Sample Exegesis

An exegesis—designed to glean information on a specific biblical passage—may include summaries, paraphrases, and direct quotes from the sources used to gain the information. Note that when a verse is quoted, the version of the Bible from which the verse was taken is identified in parentheses. Since the verse in the example is a long one and includes several important clauses, the verse is fragmented for study of the individual clauses. A numbering system helps keep the sources separated. Identifying the sources in brackets is done by noting either the author or the title of the work. In practice, a bibliography at the end of the exegesis would provide full publication data for the sources cited in the exegesis. As an example, a partial exegesis of 1 Peter 1:3 is shared below.

1 Peter 1:3: "Blessed be the God and Father of our Lord Jesus Christ, who according to His abundant mercy has begotten us again to a living hope through the resurrection of Jesus Christ from the dead" (NKJV).

Blessed be the God and Father of our Lord Jesus Christ. . .
1. God is described in a distinctive Christian way. In the Old Testament God is praised (that is the meaning here of "blessed") as Creator and as Redeemer from Egyptian bondage. Christians praise God as the Father of the Incarnate Son. Jesus is specifically described as *our* Messiah [Tyndale, p. 74].

147

2. Peter opens his epistle with sustained eloquence in which adoration, teaching, and exhortation are interwoven. "The effect is like that of some masterpiece of tapestry or a page from one of the great illuminated books of the tenth century. It arrests the attention as a whole . . ." [Selwyn, pp. 68–69].

3. Praise to God the Father is evoked by the rest of verse three *Expositor's Bible Commentary*, p. 220] "who according to His abundant mercy. . . ."

Appendix B

Sample Background Study

A background study seeks information about an entire book of the Bible. Essential in this quest is an examination of authorship, purpose, and date of the individual book. The background data could include a summary (or direct quotes) from commentaries, biblical dictionaries and encyclopedias, or any other reliable source of biblical information. An example of a partial background study on 1 Peter appears below. The sources used appear in brackets with full publication data listed in a bibliography. A numbering system is used to keep the sources separated.

Purpose of 1 Peter

1. The purpose of 1 Peter is implied at the end of the book (5:12): to encourage churches undergoing persecution. Peter assures them of the truth of their faith and encourages them to stand firm [Beare, p. 6].

2. The purpose is to fortify Christians in Asia Minor to stand fast in their loyalty to the cause of Christ in the face of severe persecution. Peter does this by reminding them of the example of Jesus on the cross, and of the heavenly inheritance of those who follow Christ [Interpreter's, p. 80].

3. Peter deals with a persecution situation. Like a good teacher, Peter urgently rams home his message in 4:12f. [Harper's, p. 10].

Appendix C

Sample Interpretation

When the background study and exegesis are completed, the preacher should make an interpretive statement that will guide sermon preparation (see chapter 3). Two examples are offered. First is the interpretive statement written by Dr. Ellis on Psalm 37:3–7. Second, a suggested interpretive statement on 1 Peter 1:3–12.

Note that the CIT in each example is stated in past tense interpreting what the text meant then; the MOT is stated in one word; the Thesis is a present tense application of the text; and the MOS is a concise statement of the desired outcome of the sermon.

Example 1

Text   Psalm 37:3–7

CIT   God promises to reward those who trust in him.

MOT   Supportive

Thesis   God promises to reward whoever trusts in him.

MOS   That the congregation will claim the rewards that God promises by trusting him.

Example 2

Text   1 Peter 1:3–12

CIT   God provided through his Son Jesus an assurance that his salvation is everlasting

MOT   Supportive

Thesis   God provides an everlasting salvation through his Son Jesus

MOS   To encourage Christians to face the struggles of life on the basis of our everlasting salvation.

Recommended Reading

See Bibliography for complete publishing data.

Chapter 1: Grasping the Fundamentals

John A. Broadus, *A Treatise in the Preparation and Delivery of Sermons*. Originally published in 1870 and revised by three other authors, this book continues to be the watershed of homiletical studies.

James Cox, *Preaching* (1985). A practical study of the nature of preaching.

Fred Craddock, *Preaching* (1985). Unique insights into the preaching task.

C. H. Dodd, *The Apostolic Preaching and Its Developments* (1936, repr. 1980). A classic work that deepens our understanding of the origins of Christian preaching.

Clyde Fant, *Preaching for Today* (1975, 1986). See chapter 5 for a superb discussion of "Incarnational Preaching."

Gene Hall and Jim Heflin, *Proclaim the Word* (1985). A philosophical introduction to preaching.

Richard Lischer, *A Theology of Preaching* (1981). An in-depth study of *why* we preach.

Robert Mounce, *The Essential Nature of New Testament Preaching* (1960). Foundational book for understanding preaching during New Testament times.

Haddon Robinson, *Biblical Preaching: The Development and Delivery of Expository Messages* (1980). An excellent source for basic homiletics.

Chapter 2: Developing Relevant Themes

Karl Barth, *Preaching Through the Christian Year* (1978). A good emphasis on the theological meaning of significant Christian Holy days.

Edgar N. Jackson, *How to Preach to People's Needs* (1970). An excellent study of how to perceive and address vital concerns of the congregation.

Chapter 3: Interpreting the Text

Frederic Farrar, *History of Interpretation* (1886, repr. 1961, 1979). This classic work on the history of hermeneutics gives the preacher a perspective on contemporary hermeneutics.

Walter Kaiser, *Toward an Exegetical Theology* (1981). A valuable resource that demonstrates how the preacher moves from biblical study to sermon construction.

Bernard Ramm, *Protestant Biblical Interpretation* (1970). A classic contemporary work that introduces the preacher to current hermeneutical approaches.

William D. Thompson, *Preaching Biblically* (1981). See chapters 2 and 3 for basic information on exegesis and interpretation.

Chapter 4: Forming the Structure

James Braga, *How to Prepare Bible Messages* (1971). See pages 139-149 for elementary discussion on preparing sermon outlines.

David Buttrick, *Homiletic* (1987). See pages 308-317 for brief discussion of structuring the sermon.

H. Grady Davis, *Design for Preaching* (1958). See pages 35–40 for a discussion of developing unity in sermon structure.

Chapter 5: Applying the Dynamics of Self-Expression

H. C. Brown, Jr., *A Quest for Reformation in Preaching* (1968). See chapter 4 for a thorough analysis of the functional elements of preaching.

Chapter 6: Evaluating the Product

H. C. Brown, Jr., *A Quest for Reformation in Preaching* (1968). See chapters 5–6 for a discussion of biblical authority as it relates to preaching.

James Earl Massey. *The Sermon in Perspective* (1976). Offers specific suggestions on how to improve sermons.

Chapter 7: Varying the Content

Harold Freeman, *Varieties in Biblical Preaching* (1987). The definitive book on various creative ways to develop a sermon.

Alton McEachern, *Dramatic Monologue Preaching* (1984). Instructive for portraying a biblical character in a sermon with several sermonic examples.

Edmund Steimle, Morris Niedenthal, Charles Rice, *Preaching the Story* (1980). Story-telling is examined as an approach to preaching.

Robert Young, *Religious Imagination* (1979). See pages 26–48 for a discussion of developing the preacher's imagination.

Chapter 8: Delivering the Message

Jon Eisenson, *Voice and Diction* (1974). A comprehensive book on voice production and diction.

Al Fasol, *A Guide to Self-Improvement in Sermon Delivery* (1983). Designed to provide immediate assistance to the pastor who needs a program of self-improvement in sermon delivery.

Dwight Stevenson, Charles Diehl, *Reaching People from the Pulpit* (1958). A dated but useful book on sermon delivery.

Chapter 9: Improving the Dynamics

Russell Dilday, *Personal Computer: A New Tool for Ministers* (1985). See pages 69–72 for information on filing sermons in a computer.

Paul Gericke, *The Minister's Filing System* (1971, 1978). Excellent suggestions for preachers who do not use a computer.

Bibliography

Aycock, Donald, ed. *Preaching with Purpose and Power.* Macon: Mercer University Press, 1982.

Armstrong, James. *Telling Truth.* Grand Rapids: Baker Book House, 1976.

Baillie, D. M. *To Whom Shall We Go?* Grand Rapids: Baker Book House, 1974.

Barth, Karl. *Deliverance to the Captives.* Translated by Marguerite Wieser. New York: Harper & Bros., 1961.

———. *The Preaching of the Gospel.* Translated by B. E. Hooke. Philadelphia: Westminster Press, 1963.

———. *Preaching Through the Christian Year.* Grand Rapids: Wm. B. Eerdmans, 1978.

———. *The Word of God and the Word of Man.* Translated by Douglas Horton. London: Hodder & Stoughton, 1928.

Blackwood, Andrew. *The Fine Art of Preaching.* Grand Rapids: Baker Book House, reprint 1976.

———. *The Preparation of Sermons.* Nashville: Abingdon, 1958.

Blum, Edwin A. *Expositor's Bible Commentary: 1 Peter.* Vol. 12. Grand Rapids: Zondervan, 1981.

Braga, James. *How to Prepare Bible Messages.* Portland, Oregon: Multnomah Press, 1971.

Broadus, John A. *A Treatise on the Preparation and Delivery of Sermons.* Revised by Jesse B. Weatherspoon. New York: Harper & Bros., 1944.

Brooks, Keith; Bahn, Eugene; Okey, L. L. *The Communicative Act of Oral Interpretation.* Boston: Allyn & Bacon, 1975.

Brooks, Phillips. *Lectures on Preaching.* London: Griffith, Farrar & Co., 1877.

Brown, H. C., Jr. *A Quest for Reformation in Preaching.* Waco: Word, 1968.

————— . *Sermon Analysis for Pulpit Power.* Nashville: Broadman, 1971.

————— . *Southern Baptist Preaching.* Nashville: Broadman, 1959.

————— , ed. *More Southern Baptist Preaching.* Nashville: Broadman, 1964.

Brown, H. C., Jr.; Clinard, H. Gordon; and Northcutt, Jesse J. *Steps to the Sermon.* Nashville: Broadman, 1963.

Bryson, Harold T., and Taylor, James C. *Building Sermons to Meet People's Needs.* Nashville: Broadman, 1980.

Buerlein, Homer K. *How to Preach More Powerful Sermons.* Philadelphia: Westminster Press, (1984) 1986.

Buttrick, David. *Homiletic.* Philadelphia: Fortress, 1987.

Claypool, John. *The Preaching Event.* Waco: Word, 1980.

Cox, James. *Biblical Preaching.* Philadelphia: Westminster Press, 1983.

————— . *Preaching.* New York: Harper & Row, 1985.

Craddock, Fred. *As One Without Authority.* Nashville, Abingdon, 1971.

————— . *Overhearing the Gospel.* Nashville: Abingdon, 1978.

————— . *Preaching.* Nashville: Abingdon, 1985.

Dargan, E. C. *A History of Preaching.* 2 vols. New York: George H. Doran Co., 1905.

Davis, H. Grady. *Design for Preaching.* Philadelphia: Muhlenberg Press, 1958.

DeBrand, Roy E. *Guide to Biographical Preaching.* Nashville: Broadman, 1983.

Dilday, Russell. *Personal Computer: A New Tool for Ministers.* Nashville: Broadman, 1985.

Dodd, C. H. *The Apostolic Preaching and Its Developments* (1936). Grand Rapids: Baker Book House, repr. 1980.

Eisenson, Jon. *Voice and Diction.* New York: Macmillan, 1974.

Erdahl, Lowell O. *Better Preaching.* St. Louis: Concordia Press, 1977.

Fant, Clyde. *Preaching for Today.* New York: Harper & Row, (1975) 1986.

Fant, Clyde, and Pinson, William. *Twenty Centuries of Great Preaching.* Waco: Word, 1971.

Farrar, Frederic. *History of Interpretation* (1886). Grand Rapids: Baker Book House, repr. 1961, 1979.

Fasol, Al. *A Guide to Self-Improvement in Sermon Delivery.* Grand Rapids: Baker Book House, 1983.

————. *Selected Readings in Preaching.* Grand Rapids: Baker Book House, 1979.

Fish, Roy. *Giving a Good Invitation.* Nashville: 1974.

Fosdick, Harry Emerson. *Riverside Sermons.* New York: Harper & Bros., 1958.

Freeman, Harold. *Varieties in Biblical Preaching.* Waco: Word, 1987.

————. *The Relevance for Preaching of Various Approaches to New Testament Studies.* (Unpublished, presented at a faculty seminar, Southwestern Baptist Theological Seminary, Fort Worth, TX, 1986.)

Fuller, Otis, ed. *Spurgeon's Lectures to His Students.* Grand Rapids: Zondervan, 1945.

Fuller, Reginald. *The Use of the Bible in Preaching.* Philadelphia: Fortress, 1981.

Gericke, Paul. *The Minister's Filing System.* 1971. Grand Rapids: Baker Book House, 1978.

Gossip, Arthur J. *The Hero in Thy Soul.* Edinburgh: T & T Clark, 1928.

Grasso, Domenico. *Proclaiming God's Message: A Study in the Theology of Preaching.* South Bend: University of Notre Dame Press, 1965.

Hall, Gene, and Heflin, Jim. *Proclaim the Word.* Nashville: Broadman, 1985.

Horne, Chevis. *Preaching the Great Themes of the Bible.* Nashville: Broadman, 1986.

Hobbs, Herschel H. *Proclaiming the New Testament: The Gospel of Matthew.* Grand Rapids: Baker Book House, 1961.

Hovland, Carl; Janis, Irving; Kelley, Harold. *Communication and Persuasion.* New Haven: Yale Univ. Press, 1953.

Jackson, Edgar N. *How to Preach to People's Needs.* Grand Rapids: Baker Book House, 1970.

Jowett, John H. *The Preacher: His Life and Work (1912).* Grand Rapids: Baker Book House, repr. 1968.

Kaiser, Walter. *Toward an Exegetical Theology.* Grand Rapids: Baker Book House, 1981.

King, Martin Luther, Jr. *Strength to Live.* Copyright 1963 by Martin Luther King, Jr.

Lenski, R. C. H. *The Sermon: Its Homiletical Construction.* (1912). Grand Rapids: Baker Book House, repr. 1968.

Lischer, Richard. *A Theology of Preaching.* Nashville: Abingdon, 1981.

Logan, Samuel, ed. *The Preacher and Preaching.* Phillipsburg: Presbyterian and Reformed Publishing Co., 1986.

Lowry, Eugene. *The Homiletical Plot.* Atlanta: John Knox Press, 1980.

Luccock, Halford E. *In the Minister's Workshop (1944).* Grand Rapids: Baker Book House, repr. 1977.

Maier, Walter A. *For Christ and Country.* St. Louis: Concordia Publishing House, 1942.

Massey, James Earl. *Designing the Sermon.* Nashville: Abingdon, 1984.

————. *The Responsible Pulpit.* Anderson, Indiana: Warner Press, 1974.

————. *The Sermon in Perspective.* Grand Rapids: Baker Book House, 1976.

McEachern, Alton. *Dramatic Monologue Preaching.* Nashville: Broadman, 1984.

Meyer, F. B. *Expository Preaching: Plans and Methods* (1913). Grand Rapids: Baker Book House, repr. 1974.

Mickelson, A. Berkley. *Interpreting the Bible.* Grand Rapids: Wm. B. Eerdmans, 1963.

Morgan, G. Campbell. *Preaching* (1955). Repr. ed., Grand Rapids: Baker Book House, 1974.

————. *The Westminster Pulpit.* Vol. VIII. Westwood, N.J.: Fleming H. Revell, n.d.

Morris, Calvin. *The Word and the the Words.* Nashville: Abingdon, 1975.

Mounce, Robert. *The Essential Nature of New Testament Preaching*. Grand Rapids: Wm. B. Eerdmans, 1960.

Newport, John, and Cannon, William. *Why Christians Fight Over the Bible*. Nashville: Thomas Nelson, 1974.

Newton, Joseph F. *The New Preaching*. Nashville: Cokesbury, 1930.

Nichols, J. Randall. *Building the Word*. New York: Harper & Row, 1980.

————. *Preaching as Pastoral Communication*. New York: Harper & Row, 1987.

Parker, Joseph. *Ad Clerum: Advices to a Young Preacher*. Boston: Roberts Brothers, 1871.

Ramm, Bernard. *Protestant Biblical Interpretation*. Grand Rapids: Baker Book House, 1970.

Robertson, Frederick W. *Sermons on Bible Subjects*. New York: E. P. Dutton, 1906.

Robinson, Haddon. *Biblical Preaching: The Development and Delivery of Expository Messages*. Grand Rapids: Baker Book House, 1980.

Rossow, Francis C. *Preaching the Active Gospel Actively*. St. Louis: Concordia Publishing House, 1983.

Scherer, Paul. *For We Have This Treasure*. New York: Harper & Row, 1944.

————. *The Word of God Sent*. Grand Rapids: Baker Book House, 1965.

Selwyn, E. G. *The First Epistle of St. Peter*. London: MacMillan & Co., 1947.

Shoemaker, Samuel. *The Church Alive*. New York: E.P. Dutton, 1950.

Sluth, Ronald. *God's Word and Our Words*. Atlanta: John Knox Press, 1986.

Smart, James. *The Interpretation of Scripture*. Philadelphia: Westminster Press, 1961.

Sperry, Willard L. *Sermons Preached at Harvard*. New York: Harper & Bros., 1953.

Spurgeon, Charles H. *Spurgeon's Lectures to His Students*. Edited by D. O. Fuller. Grand Rapids: Zondervan, 1956.

Steimle, Edmund; Niedenthal, Morris; and Rice, Charles. *Preaching the Story*. Philadelphia: Fortress, 1980.

Stevenson, Dwight, and Diehl, Charles. *Reaching People from the Pulpit*. New York: Harper & Row, 1958.

Stewart, James S. *A Faith to Proclaim*. New York: Scribner's Sons, 1953.

———. *Heralds of God*. London: Hodder & Stoughton, 1946.

Stibbs, Alan M. *Tyndale New Testament Commentaries: The First Epistle General of Peter*. Grand Rapids: Wm. B. Eerdmans, (1959) 1981.

Stott, John R. *Between Two Worlds*. Grand Rapids: Wm. B. Eerdmans, 1982.

———. *The Preacher's Portrait*. Grand Rapids: Wm. B. Eerdmans, 1982.

———. *The Preacher's Portrait in the New Testament*. Grand Rapids: Wm. B. Eerdmans, 1961.

Thielieke, Helmut. *The Waiting Father*. New York: Harper & Row, 1959.

Thompson, William D. *Preaching Biblically*. Nashville: Abingdon, 1981.

Young, Robert. *Religious Imagination*. Philadelphia: Westminster Press, 1979.

Notes

Chapter 1

1. Phillips Brooks, *Lectures on Preaching* (London: Griffith, Farrar & Co., 1877), p. 5.

2. E. C. Dargan, *A History of Preaching* (New York: George H. Doran Co., 1905), vol. I, ch. 1.

3. Examples of sermons in every era of Christian preaching are available in *Twenty Centuries of Great Preaching,* edited by Clyde Fant and William Pinson (Waco: Word, 1971).

4. H. C. Brown, Jr., H. Gordon Clinard, and Jesse J. Northcutt, *Steps to the Sermon* (Nashville: Broadman, 1963), p. 25.

5. *Ibid.,* p. 26.

6. Clyde Fant, *Preaching for Today* (New York: Harper & Row, 1975), p. 1.

7. John Newport and William Cannon, *Why Christians Fight Over The Bible* (Nashville: Thomas Nelson, 1974), p. 16.

8. Charles H. Spurgeon, *Spurgeon's Lectures to His Students* (Grand Rapids: Zondervan, 1956), p. 42.

Chapter 2

1. H. C. Brown, Jr., H. Gordon Clinard, and Jesse J. Northcutt, *Steps to the Sermon* (Nashville: Broadman, 1963), p. 34.

2. Samuel Shoemaker, *The Church Alive* (New York: E. P. Dutton, 1950), p. 63.

3. Homer K. Buerlein, *How To Preach More Powerful Sermons* (Philadelphia: Westminster Press, 1984), p. 26.

4. Helmut Thielicke, *The Waiting Father* (New York: Harper & Row, 1959), pp. 17–18.

5. R. C. H. Lenski, *The Sermon: Its Homiletical Construction* (1927. Grand Rapids: Baker Book House, reprinted 1968), p. 12.

Chapter 3

1. John A. Broadus, *A Treatise On the Preparation and Delivery of Sermons*, rev. ed. by Jesse B. Weatherspoon (New York: Harper & Bros., 1944), p. 24.

2. Harold Freeman, *The Relevance for Preaching of Various Approaches to New Testament Studies* (Unpublished, presented at a faculty seminar, Southwestern Baptist Theological Seminary, 1986.)

Chapter 4

1. Willard L. Sperry, *Sermons Preached at Harvard* (New York: Harper & Bros., 1953), p. 45.

2. Walter A. Maier, *For Christ and Country* (St. Louis: Concordia Publishing House, 1942), p. 189.

3. Arthur J. Gossip, *The Hero in Thy Soul* (Edinburgh: T & T Clark, 1928), p. 106.

4. Clyde Fant and William Pinson, *20 Centuries of Great Preaching,* Vol. XI (Waco: Word Publishers, 1971), p. 250.

5. Martin Luther King, Jr., *Strength to Live* Copyright 1963 by Martin Luther King, Jr., p. 118.

6. Frederick W. Robertson, *Sermons on Bible Subjects* (New York: E. P. Dutton & Co., 1906), pp. 116–117.

7. Herschel H. Hobbs, *Proclaiming the New Testament: The Gospel of Matthew* (Grand Rapids: Baker Book House, 1961), pp. 13–16.

8. John A. Broadus, *A Treatise on the Preparation and Delivery of Sermons* (New York: George H. Doran Co., 1898), pp. 298–299.

9. D. M. Baillie, *To Whom Shall We Go?* (Grand Rapids: Baker Book House, 1974), p. 29.

10. Roy Fish, *Giving a Good Invitation* (Nashville: Broadman, 1974), pp. 7-8.

Chapter 5

1. H. C. Brown, Jr. *A Quest for Reformation in Preaching* (Waco: Word, 1968), p. 57.

2. H. C. Brown, Jr. (ed.), *More Southern Baptist Preaching* (Nashville: Broadman, 1964), p. 134.

3. Brown, *A Quest for Reformation in Preaching,* op. cit., p. 66.

4. Harry Emerson Fosdick, *Riverside Sermons* (New York: Harper & Bros., 1958), pp. 28–37.

5. See, for example, "The Effects of the Use of Analogy in Attitude Change and Source Credibility," *Journal of Communication* 19 (Dec. 1969): pp. 333-339.

6. H. C. Brown, Jr. (ed.), *Southern Baptist Preaching* (Nashville: Broadman, 1959), p. 52.

7. Ibid., p. 67.

Chapter 6

1. See H. C. Brown, Jr. *A Quest for Reformation in Preaching,* (Waco: Word, 1968), pp. 89–90. Many of these concepts were developed by Brown in conjunction with several homilectic students, of which I was one. Brown acknowledges our assistance in his preface.

2. See G. Campbell Morgan, *The Westminster Pulpit* (Westwood, N.J.: Fleming H. Revell, n.d.), VIII, pp. 48–60.

3. Dr. Ellis is a member of the Old Testament department of the faculty of Southwestern Baptist Theological Seminary. In the preparation of this sermon, Dr. Ellis incorporated each of the steps to sermon preparation that we have studied thus far and this serves, it is hoped, as a helpful example.

Chapter 7

1. Charles H. Spurgeon, *Lectures,* p. 293.

2. Edmund Steimle, Morris Niedenthal, Charles Rice. *Preaching the Story.* (Philadelphia: Fortress, 1980), p. 14.

3. Harold Freeman, *Varieties in Biblical Preaching* (Waco: Word, 1987), pp. 157–158.

4. Ibid., p. 172.

Chapter 8

1. Al Fasol, *A Guide to Self-Improvement in Sermon Delivery* (Grand Rapids: Baker Book House, 1983), p. 9.

2. Ibid., pp. 25–39. For a detailed description of the vocal organs and the vocalization process, see Jon Eisenson, *Voice and Diction* (New York: Macmillan, 1974).

Chapter 9

1. A centennial history of the First Baptist Church of Seymour, Texas, published privately in 1984, is a model of a readable and informative history of a local church. Future pastors will find it a treasure that will enhance their preaching ministry.

2. This section is taken from an article I wrote for *Church Administration*, November 1987. Copyright 1987, the Sunday School Board of the Southern Baptist Convention. All rights reserved. Used by permission.

3. C. Welten Gaddy preached on this subject in a chapel service at Southwestern Baptist Theological Seminary on September 7, 1983. An audiotape of his superb sermon is available at Roberts Library of Southwestern.

Scripture Index

Genesis

Book of—52
6:4a—92

Exodus

20:3—55
20:7—93
20:15—93

Leviticus

14:1–2—92

Deuteronomy

18:14–22—13
32:43—46

Judges

20:25—90

Nehemiah

8:8—14

2 Chronicles

Book of—52

1 Samuel

17:40—96
17:49—92

2 Samuel

12—81

1 Kings

18:17–19, 20–24, 29,
    38–39—36
19:4—64

Job

Book of—53
5:7—63
12–14—36
13:20–22—36
16:4—62

Psalms

Book of—53
1—35
2:7—46
10—35
22:22—46
23—34
37—98
37:1–7—99, 100
37:3–7—151
46—35
50:10—85
55—34
73—34, 91
103—34
121—35

139—35
142:4—34

Proverbs

Book of—53

Ecclesiastes

Book of—53

Song of Songs

Book of—53

Isaiah

8:14—46
8:17–18—46
26:18—46
28:16—46
29:13—45, 47
56:7—47

Jeremiah

7:11—47
12:5—62

Lamentations

5:21—62

Hosea

14:2—85

Subject Index

Catachresis, 85
Central Idea of the Text, *see*
  Sermon, developing
  structure, CIT
Chaplain, military, 136–38
Christian fellowship, as spiritual
  preparation, 23–24
Chrysostom, 16, 20, 104
Clement of Alexandria, 16, 48
Clement of Rome, 16
Combination biblical authority of
  sermon, 94–96
Commentaries, 51–52, 59
Comparison, 76
Composite quotations, 47
Conclusion of sermon, 61, 66–68
Content of sermon, 103–13
Continuity of preaching, 19
Creed, 48
Creedal interpretation of scripture,
  49
Criticism, form, 44; redaction, 44;
  source, 43
Cross references, 75, 140
Cultural setting of text, 53

Daily preparation, 24–26
Dark Ages, 17
Deductive study, 51
Definitions of preaching, 15–16
Delivery, *see* Sermon delivery
Demythologizing, 50
Dialogue sermon, 111–12
Direct biblical authority of sermon,
  90–91
Distractions, 134
Dominic, 17
Donne, John 18
Dramatic monologue, 104–6

Edict of Nantes, 18
Edwards, Jonathan, 18
Eligius, 17
Ellis, Bob, 97, 151
Emphasis, vocal, 125–26
Eras
  Modern, 19
  Patristic, 16–17

Post-Reformation, 18
Pre-Reformation, 17–18
Progress, 19
Reformation, 17
Scholastic, 17
Euphemism, 85
Evaluation of sermon, 89–101,
  129–131
Exegesis, 51; sample of, 147–48;
  textual contribution to, 54
Exegetical paraphrasing, 47
Exhortation, 78
Existentialism, 50
Explanation, *see* Functional
  elements of preaching
Exposition, 75
Eye contact, 124

Facial expressions, 122
Fant, Clyde, 21
Fenelon, 18, 20
Figurative speech, 84–85
Filing sermons, 140–42
Finney, Charles G., 19, 20, 79
Fish, Roy, 69
Flashes of inspiration, 32
Form criticism, 44
Fosdick, Harry Emerson, 78, 79
Fragmentary quotes, 46
Francis of Assisi, 17, 104
Freeman, Harold, 43, 110
Frelinghuysen, Theodore, 18
Full vocal production, 115–17
Functional elements of preaching,
  71, 73–87
  Application, 77–78
  Argumentation, 79–82
  Explanation, 73–76
  General guidelines, 86–87
  Illustration, 82–86
Funeral sermons, 138–40

General guidelines, *see* Functional
  elements of preaching
Gestures, 123
Graham, Billy, 19, 20, 69, 79,
  85–86
Grammar of original biblical